A MANUAL FOR POSITIVE PRESS RELATIONS

GETTING CHURCH NEWS INTO LOCAL PAPERS

MIKE STICKLAND

Mike Stickland writes with the experience of having served as Regional and as National Communication director of his church in the UK. He is also the author of ***'Coping with Cancer and Chemo—a personal encounter'*** and ***'No Mask Required—Have You got the face to be a Christian?'***

GETTING CHURCH NEWS INTO LOCAL PAPERS

Section One: Know Your Goal!

Chapter One:

The Purpose and Objectives of PR Work and Media Contact

It does feel good to see your church featured in the local newspaper. Few would argue with that. It is gratifying when a positive impression is created by a photo or news story published straight out of your church's activities. Everyone likes to see themselves in print, including church members!

But the purpose of PR work and media contact on behalf of the church is not just to stimulate personal satisfaction for ourselves, nor even a 'warm fuzzy feeling' among the members. It would be disappointing if that was the limit of our motivation. There are more substantial reasons—sound evangelistic (dare we say 'marketing'?) reasons—to pursue PR work, which make it more than an end in itself. Efforts of the local church communication secretary can legitimately be visualized as a component of the Matthew 28 'Commission' to take the Gospel to the world.

Having said that, news reports by the church in the media rarely seem to have any immediately measurable impact in terms of drawing 'x' number of people off the streets into church attendance. Because 'results' may be hard to observe or quantify, there is a tendency to dismiss communication work as little more than a token role with nominal value. That would be even more disappointing.

Good communication does have incalculable potential in the long term for the overall purposes of the church. So we do need to recognize certain very clear incentives for approaching the communication task with vision, vigour and conviction.

The absence of regular public information about the church, limits the significance of that church to their public. If the people in your community hear little about your church, you can hardly blame them if they classify it as irrelevant.

On the other hand, the presence of lively church items in the local press raises the profile of the church. It gives birth to an awareness that behind those walls which seem excluding, impersonal and grey, a thriving church family exists, composed of real people who have a great time together.

Simply being reported positively by the public media lends a credibility which suggests relevance.

If churches remain aloof from the secular press because they feel that it would be unfruitful to do otherwise, or if they timidly hide behind the excuse that the media are indifferent to them, they will rapidly find themselves ignored. They need to register a relevance to society by consistently demonstrating their activity within society.

> ***'If the church is going to prepare large numbers of people for productive personal contacts, it must reach them through the press, making them aware of the church's existence, arousing interest in its faith and programme.'***
>
> Howard Weeks in 'Breakthrough'.

The press cannot report or publicize something of which it is ignorant or only partly informed but does not have the time to pursue.

Editors and newsrooms depend on 'informers'—people who tip them off about events and stories. It isn't good enough to *assume* that they will hear about it. You have to tell them. And even if they are aware of a particular event, they may lack the personnel to send a reporter to every story. Consequently editors depend upon material being brought to them in an interesting and ready-to-use format. This is where local communication secretaries come into their own.

Many an editor will appreciate it when the communication secretary takes the initiative and submits a news release. What is presented should require the minimum of fuss or additional work to include it in the next edition. If the editor sees the prospect of much more mileage out of the story, then (and usually only then) he will dispatch a reporter in your direction.

When we take the initiative, we are more likely to get an accurate report which correctly expresses our point of view.

Busy reporters, rushing from one assignment to the next, will be glad for a pithy news release to help them grasp the story from your perspective. They may have little personal religious background by which to appreciate your story. Their day may have been heavily affected by all kinds of other news items, which may influence how they perceive yours. So it is important that communication secretaries ensure that their items are presented truthfully and attractively, incorporating a positive Christian perspective. As a result, one can expect that what is published will be pleasing to all parties.

Press relations activity provokes and improves the performance of the church

As a church sees its items published by the local media, so it is stimulated to make sure that it lives up to the high standards of the image presented. This stimulates the church towards its own ideal because it is now on public record as having a particular set of standards, perspectives or priorities. It should be seen to be true to that image or will risk being discredited. The church is forced to take a more comprehensive look at its wider image, and to think more seriously about how its community perceives it.

Consistently good and regular PR is an essential, integral component in the early stages of productive evangelism.

The human mind goes through elaborate processes in order to arrive at a decision.

Take something as simple as buying a box of detergent. It is not just a matter of picking one off the supermarket shelf at random. There have been considerable influences at work before we make our decision, some of which have been conscious, and others subconscious.

The distinct steps in the process of decision-making have been identified as:

•Awareness
•Interest
•Evaluation
•Trial
•Adoption.

First we need to become aware that a given product exists. We need to know something about what it does and how it will help us. Once we know that it is on the market, we may look out for it or seek to find out more information. An interest in the product germinates in our mind.

If sufficiently interested, we may move on to evaluate the merits of the product, and then try it for ourselves—test drive it, if you like. Does it do everything the manufacturer claims? Is it as good as they say it is? If we become convinced that it is a good product and that the benefit justifies the cost, we may adopt or purchase the product.

If we have never heard of a product, nor never tested its claims, we are not likely to commit ourselves heavily to it.

Consider what happens when we buy life insurance. We may hear from a close friend that a particular company offers a good deal, but if we have never heard of that company or its product, we are likely to hesitate. If, on the other hand, we have seen the company and its product advertised several times and have read good reports in the media, we attach a credibility to it which is merely confirmed by the recommendation of our friend.

The same principle applies when someone makes up their mind about becoming a Christian or going along to a particular church. They won't—unless something has previously confirmed the value and integrity of that faith or that congregation. We should not assume that the whole story begins at the point when the evangelist appeals for a decision. In fact it is more usual that a long history of influences gradually, imperceptibly, created a context in which that ultimate positive response was possible.

When someone expresses the belief that his church is 'the place to be', the invitation to come along and see for oneself will only be taken seriously if there is already a positive image accumulating in the sub-conscious mind.

This suggests that there is a legitimate role for the communication secretary, within an overall evangelistic framework, to present items to the media so that a confidence is encouraged in the mind of the receiver.

In this way, the communication secretary is involved in the earliest stages of introducing a member of the public to what the church has to offer.

Other reasons for a sustained PR programme can be listed:

- It provides a means of reaching people who never go near a church.
- Items published by the secular media stand a high chance of being read because people tend to read their local newspapers thoroughly.
- Your 'good' news item can compensate to some extent for the normal diet of gloom and doom.
- It puts the name of your church into people's minds.
- It promotes credibility for Christianity in the public mind by letting people know that the church exists and is alive and has relevant views and activities.

SUMMARY:

When communication secretaries formulate clear reasons and objectives for implementing an on-going PR programme, their work will have shape and purpose that will motivate them to strive for the highest of standards. It will contain the seeds of gradual success. □□

Section One: Know Your Goal!

Chapter Two:

Know Your Congregation and its 'Mission Statement'.

It may seem a silly question with an obvious answer, but why does your church exist? In 'wayside pulpit' language, 'What on earth is your church here for?' Or put more academically, 'What is its raison d'etre—its reason for being'?

The buzz phrase is probably 'What is your Mission Statement?' The expression is used widely in commerce and industry nowadays to clarify the marketing objectives of a company. In this context, 'mission' does not have a religious meaning as such, but simply refers to the objectives of the organisation, secular or religious. Richard Thomas refers to the mission statement as a 'communication aim'.

> ***'A communication aim is a statement about what is to be achieved with a particular programme or communication project, and it is used to measure the success or failure of the communication programme. A good communication aim is usually short, sharp and specific. It says what is to be done, why it's to be done, and for how long. It should be agreed by the church, or group, on whose behalf the work is being done, and it should be realistic and achievable within the resources of time and money available.'***
>
> **Richard Thomas in 'An Introduction to Church Communication'**

*The question does need to be asked—**'Why does our congregation exist?'** Answering it ensures that realistic corporate aspirations are understood and agreed by all parties. Not least, the local church communication secretary needs to know, understand and identify with the 'mission statement' of the church so that he/she will be in a position to develop a 'communication aim' and set about liaising with the local media appropriately.*

This chapter seeks to help with the task of knowing your church and understanding its objectives.

Agreeing a 'Mission Statement' for the local church.

It may seem difficult to get this self-assessment started. People sometimes react defensively and need to be reassured that the questions do not imply criticism if answered one way, or approval if answered another. No value judgements are being made. The aim is merely to recognise the potential and the limitations of your given congregation, and thereby to agree what attainable objectives you may have.

The tactful way to approach the matter is to raise it first on an informal basis with the pastor. Ask whether he might take 10 minutes during a church board meeting to float some tentative questions, with a view to a conclusive discussion and democratic definition at the subsequent meeting

The following list may help prepare questions suited to your local context. They are not given in any sense of priority.

- Is our church a place where we desire simply to come aside together for mutual fellowship, to praise the Lord and gain spiritual comfort without the aggravation of the world interfering with us or impinging upon us?

OR:

- Is our church a facility we perceive as both a place for worship and a base for operation of a programme which is to be as dynamic and proactive as our members can manage under God? Is it a place from which we seek to take God's solutions into the world?

- What potential can we identify, and what limitations impose themselves on our congregation, by virtue of:

  - our numbers;
  - their age;
  - their proximity to our church in terms of where they live and work;
  - their domestic or professional commitments;
  - the facilities of our building;
  - the disposition of members towards high involvement with a church programme?

- Is our church essentially a retreat from the world, or a bridgehead into the world? Do we actually want the world knocking at our door for answers?

- Do we deeply <u>want</u> to interface with our community? Do we actually wish for interaction with society? Do we have a disposition to make an impact on the public?

Is there presently anything in our programme that succeeds in achieving those kinds of goals?

- Do we demonstrate as a congregation that we would prefer to be left alone by our community and the media, to follow our own agenda in privacy?

- Is our 'bottom line' a desire to have proactive interaction with our community on their terms—to be a 'community dynamo' type of church?

  OR:

- Is it to follow our beliefs as best we can, and if the world wants interaction they will need to come to us on our terms—a 'quiet haven' type of church?

The fact is that many congregations do have limitations by virtue of the composition, age, distribution and proximity of its membership. Whilst on principle most congregations would like to be out-going, and would be loath to relinquish or abandon that attitude, in reality they may have little choice. Therefore it is no disgrace to acknowledge the way things are, and adjust aspirations accordingly.

Recognition of the actual profile of your church helps the communication secretary enormously. It will protect you from feeling guilty if you do not seem to have as much news as a neighbouring or sister church.

The 'quiet haven' type of congregation is not likely to have so much happening within its walls that is of newsworthy interest to a local editor. It will still have occasional items, but these will be of a different nature and frequency than those of the 'community dynamo' style of church.

Mission statements tend to evolve. The first draft is often too vague, too unspecified, and will need to be tightened up. You might begin with a broad declaration such as:

'We want people to know we are here and what we stand for.'

That is a reasonable starting point, but is not specific enough. It needs to have a time-frame. It needs to define who 'people' are. It needs to say something more about why? and how?

Version 2 might then evolve: **'During the next twelve months, we would like to reach the people who live in the community of our church so that they come to know of us as a caring church.'**

This has added some flesh to the bones, but still doesn't go far enough. Do we really want them just to *know about* us? Do we not want to include them by providing programmes that will encourage them to be involved with us too? We have to define the desired result!

We want to create an attractive and relevant image of ourselves in the minds of families in our community. We want to pass on affirmative information about who we are and what makes us tick. We want to leave an open invitation in their minds which in due course they will feel relaxed about taking up.

For example, perhaps the church has a number of senior citizens who would appreciate a day-centre to come once or twice a week for a meal and social mix. They know of others in the town who would appreciate the same. The church has a number of people capable of organising the catering and entertainment, so the decision is made to launch a 'Golden Days Club'.

Or perhaps the church has a number of children who enjoy getting together for organised activities. The Pathfinder Club sees opportunities of providing a service to other children in the housing estate neighbouring the church.

So the final version of our communication aim might read something like:

'During the next twelve months, we want to communicate with people of the town, so as to create interest in our activities for both senior and junior citizens, and encourage them to come along too.'

Knowing your church and your news sources.

Reporters on your local newspaper have a 'beat' which they work in order to cull stories and news. This may be the local courts of law, the local council, local sports clubs, or something similar. To be successful they must cultivate their contacts and tune them to the needs of the paper.

In the same way, the local communication secretary needs to develop a sense of a parish 'beat' that they must nurture. This will consist of the various departments of the church and its leaders. Through regular contact, these people will get to know what kind of information you are on the lookout for, and they may even begin to take the initiative and contact you.

In the context of your mission statement and communication aim, talk with the church leaders frequently to enable mutual fulfilment of the goal. Don't just leave it to them to come to you! You must regularly ask what plans and programmes they have in the pipeline, so that you can anticipate a newsworthy story. This is where your diary comes into play.

Is a special guest visiting soon? What background information can you find on them to help you shape a news release? Is there an event scheduled that will provide a news story?

Think laterally. Keep measuring your 'mission statement' against the 'profile of newsworthiness' and make use of every opportunity to utilise your local paper in your communication aim. □□

Section Two: Setting Up Shop

Chapter Three:

The System and Equipment of PR Work and Media Contact

Effective PR doesn't just happen. It is achieved by people who approach the task systematically. It involves method and consistency. It demands the potential to respond to a crisis, as well as to commit creative energy to the routine. It deserves punctuality and thoroughness in meeting media deadlines.

It also requires access to some basic hardware and software. Many church boards will opt to appoint a communication secretary who already possesses such equipment, has keyboard skills, and a creative and willing disposition for the demands of the role. Otherwise they may need to consider sanctioning the acquisition of such equipment against the church PR budget, which items would remain the property of the church and be transferred to any subsequent incumbent.

We could summarize these essentials under the following headings: Time; System; Hardware; Software. As Richard Thomas has put it, ***'Good communication costs time, money and energy. Bad communication wastes time, money and energy.'***

TIME: Time is of the essence for effective PR. It is not that we are talking of several hours relentlessly given every week, but of the need to commit time when the necessity or opportunity arises.

Thus, if a local church is looking for a competent communication programme it should select a PR secretary who has the capacity to be imaginative and who is willing to commit sufficient time. The old adage *'If you want something done, ask a busy person'* suggests that this does not necessarily mean the church should appoint someone who has lots of uncommitted time on their hands.

The critical factors are:

- ***The aptitude*** to consistently use one's mind and creativity;
- ***The attitude*** to visualize news opportunities;
- ***The allocation*** of sufficient time to execute an effective plan.

Reluctant communication secretaries are probably going to fail, no matter how much 'time' they appear to have on their hands. It is the willingness, the commitment and the vision that count.

SYSTEM: Effective communication is all about anticipation. It anticipates news possibilities. It anticipates the kind of information that will need to be to hand, such as names and addresses of personnel. It anticipates media deadlines. It anticipates the need to work systematically.

- **Start a diary.**

Buy a decent-sized edition which includes a year-planner so that you can visualize opportunities and deadlines in advance. Write into the diary details of the church calendar including national or regional events. The pastor will usually have received a copy of this some months before the year commences. Ask him for a copy. Add all known local events which relate to your church programme.

Take the diary with you whenever you are at church or when you are involved in a church activity or planning committee. Ask the various leaders in the church for dates of their special events and programmes, and include them all in the diary.

- **Establish a dedicated address book or database.**

Include in it the names, addresses and phone numbers of current local church officers, the pastor, regional and national church office details and personnel, and media contacts including local press editors, local religious radio presenters and producers. A phone call to the switchboard of local newspaper and radio offices will give you the information you need.

You might wish to include details of professionals in related fields such as sign-writers, printers, poster-makers, advertising agencies, distribution agencies, photographers, photographic processors, etc.

- **Compile a list of media deadlines.**

Contact editors or the newsrooms of local newspapers, and religious programme producers in local radio, for a list of their deadlines. Record this information in a convenient way for quick reference. It is essential information you will need to have at your fingertips.

- **Set up a filing system.**

More about files and their contents later, but to begin with, set yourself up with some form of filing system. The most basic is a cardboard box which you can section off into different categories, but your local PR budget ought to allow you to purchase at least one of the manila concertina-style files.

As you advance in the assignment, you may get to the place when you could use a proper filing cabinet, but this is probably only for the long-term enthusiast!

- **Start some scrapbooks.**

These will help you in a couple of ways. First they may spark off a positive idea for your own reportage, and second they may warn you of what to avoid. Copycat items are not of much interest to editors, but successful styles and presentations provide good patterns for the future.

Set up one scrapbook to contain clippings of all church or religious news items published in your local papers. Set up another for clippings of your own stories published in local papers. Be sure to identify the date and details of publication for each item. You may need a third in which you can paste clippings of your stories that get published in your own national church paper.

Plan to preserve these scrapbooks and pass them on to your successor because they will become a valuable reference.

- **Build a basic library.**

Books and other printed resources are vital tools in the hands of a creative communication secretary.

You are going to need a dictionary, so invest in a good one. You will also benefit from a thesaurus to help you find alternative words to say the same thing to introduce variety into the 'copy' that you submit for publication. If you have a word-processor, most software packages now have a dictionary and thesaurus resident in the program. Do use them! It is a simple step to get your machine to do these checks, and some will even check your grammar for you at the same time.

Good books on Christian journalism, written with the lay person in mind, are available from high street book shops. If your budget will permit it, try at least to purchase:

'Breakthrough—A Public Relations Guidebook for Your Church' by Howard Weeks, and published by the Review & Herald Publishing Association, Washington DC., USA.

'Keep In Touch—A practical guide to help churches improve their communications' by Peter Crumpler and published by Scripture Union (UK). 1993.

'An Introduction To Church Communication' by Richard Thomas and published by Lynx Communications, (UK) 1994.

'The UK Christian Handbook' published annually by MARC (Europe) is a good tool for the more serious communication secretary who envisages developing the assignment over a sustained period.

'Crisis Management—What to Do When the Unthinkable Happens' by Michael Regester, and published by Hutchinson Business, (UK) 1990.

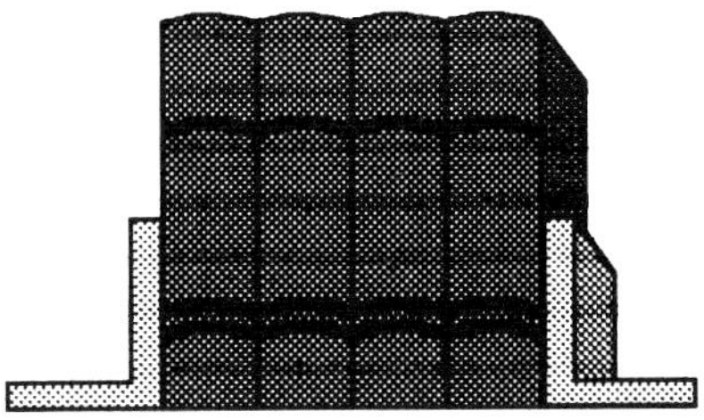

- **Use your local library.**

If you do not subscribe to local newspapers, you must avail yourself of the opportunity to read them regularly.

It is usually possible to read local daily and evening papers at your library. The importance of being familiar with local papers is that you will need to have a 'feel' for the kind of material they publish.

The library will also have other resources, such as copies of **Benn's Media Directory** which provides details of publishers and addresses of all newspapers and periodicals published within the UK. As a local communication secretary, you are unlikely to need to contact national media, but if you know where to find the contact addresses, it will be helpful.

- **Subscribe to the national (or international) church paper of your denomination.**

You need to know what your own church is doing world-wide. Your budget should underwrite this subscription. Enquire about other official news bulletins issued by your denomination, and obtain regular copies if available.

HARDWARE: The primary tool of the communication secretary is the typewriter or word-processor. Hand-written submissions to a local editor are prime candidates for the bin!

There is a time and place for hand-written letters, but news releases must be typed. So beg, buy or borrow something suitable. A modest word-processor is the best choice of the 90s because they are so flexible and do so much of the work for you.

You will need a telephone.

You may need a camera, but most often the editor of the local press will prefer to send his own photographer. Pictures submitted by 'amateurs' are rarely used in newspapers except in a 'scoop' situation. Visit the editor to confirm what kind of photos he can use with your reports. This will save mutual disappointment!

A radio that will receive local FM broadcasts is an asset because this will enable you to tune in to local religious and news programmes. Familiarity with those programmes will enable you to know what kind of items you might successfully bring to their attention. Most BBC local radio stations broadcast some form of religious Sunday morning breakfast show, whose producers are very open to approaches from churches in their catchment area. Some will send a team to record a service at your church, if the service is formatted with their listeners in mind.

Access to a photocopier is almost indispensable. Many churches now have them on-site. Public libraries and many corner shops offer a copying service. Carbon copies are no longer popular, but if that is the only convenient option, use it.

SOFTWARE: This category covers the basic stationery you will need for the job. This should include:
A4 white bond paper
Pens, pencils, eraser, ruler;
Note pad;
Envelopes and stamps;
Church letterhead if available;
Film for camera.

The category also includes a logbook in which to record your endeavours and successes. This is important from a personal audit perspective. It will help you improve and modify your work in the future, and will also enable you to prepare your reports to the church.

Keep a record of the number of stories you submit to the media, the number they print, the number of pictures they publish, and the length of your published items in column inches (or centimetres). Include details of every submission, whether it is a success or a failure.

Footnote on Files:

We have already noted the need for an effective filing system. One of the concertina-envelope styles of manila file should be more than adequate to get rolling. As the system develops it will benefit from having these categories included:

♦ Local media file to include details of contact numbers, personnel, deadlines, publishing or broadcasting times and days.

♦ Profiles file in which you keep a record of some personal information of the pastor, local church leaders and members, such as the names of their families, occupations, hobbies, birth dates. This is to provide you with resource information at short notice for any story you submit.

♦ Photo file—more difficult to assemble, but if you can accumulate good black and white photos of the pastor and local leaders, of the church building and of the church family at worship, these may prove indispensable.

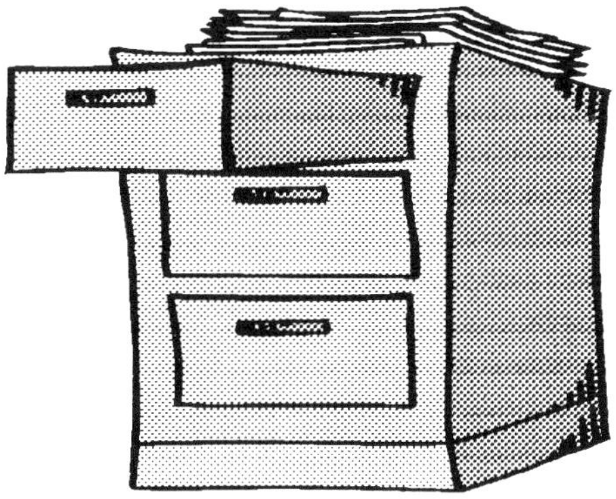

♦ Clippings file into which you drop copies of all your published articles. Record the date, newspaper and any other vital reference information with the clipping.

♦ Ideas file which should hold examples of all sorts of stories other people have published, and notes of ideas and forth-coming events that you think you may cover.

♦ Religious news file. It is often helpful to have copies of all religious news items that has been published by local and national media, of any church or religion. This will provide background information, ideas, resources.

♦ Local church department file. This may be sectionalised, and would contain notes of all activities, plans and programmes for future reference. As someone has said, 'It might come in handy, even if we never use it!'

- Institutional file to retain all papers issued from the regional or national administrative office of your church.

- Reports file to preserve copies of all reports you submit to central office or local church.

- Denominational publications file to build a complete set of your national or international church paper(s) for future reference.

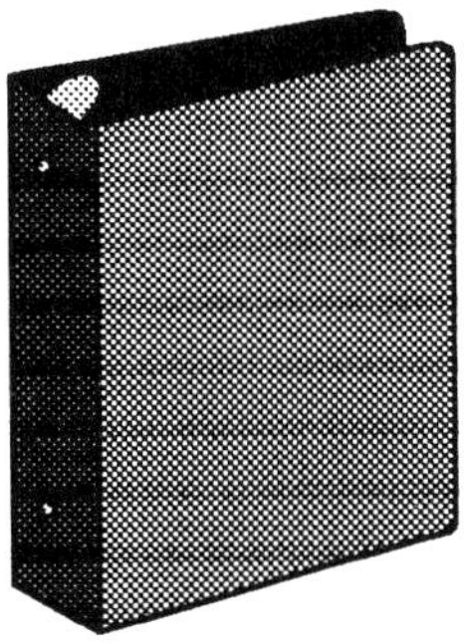

- Local issues file in which you drop clippings from the local press of various issues in the community that may even remotely be of interest for your church to make comment or contribute towards the debate. This would include matters relating to religious liberty, Christian standards, Sunday trading, crime, moral integrity in public service, family life, etc.

Section Two: Setting Up Shop

Chapter Four:

Know Your Local Media

A certain PR consultant, working for his church at national level, was invited to assist the churches in one city as they prepared the way for a city-wide evangelistic mission. One local communication secretary met him at the railway station to drive him to his hotel, and en route made the comment, 'We're really glad you've come! We've been waiting for you to introduce us to the newspaper editors.' 'You've been waiting for me to introduce you?' he quizzed, 'I anticipated that you would introduce them to me!'

One of the most frequent stumbling blocks to effective PR work and media contact is that local church communication secretaries fail to take the initiative to get to know local media personnel. Perhaps they are intimidated at the thought of knocking at the door or making that first telephone call. Admittedly the prospect of talking face-to-face with a newspaper editor or a local radio producer is somewhat daunting, because we know they are professionals and we are amateurs.

But this need not be so. The classic concept of a hard-bitten journalist who has no time for 'do-gooders' is little more than a phoney caricature. In the majority of cases you will find people just like yourself. They are busy, but they are also men and women who work for media which are hungry for material. They will be glad of your call, and even if they do not use your first story, at least now they will know who to contact and how to reach you for subsequent news stories.

This chapter is all about gearing up for effective PR work and media contact by familiarising yourself with the media institutions and personnel with whom you will work. We will look at it in two sections:

- *Researching the bare facts and data about local media in terms of what is there, who to contact and how they operate; and*

- *Researching the living realities of what they will publish and how to establish productive contact with them.*

Assembling initial data about what media are available in the area, whom to contact within that media, and how they operate. Central public libraries keep lists of newspaper publishers and local radio stations. Otherwise local council information offices can help. Failing that, refer to

Benns Media Directory or **Willings Press Guide**, on the shelf in the reference section of the library. Prepare a card-file or information sheet for each, to include:

* Name, address, phone and fax numbers;
* Circulation information such as publication day, frequency of publication, news deadline, circulation size and area;
* Personnel information such as names and contact details for Editor, News Editor, Features Editor, Religious news Editor.

Remember that you are only collating information about local or regional media. Generally speaking you will not need to communicate with national media, since this will be in the hands of the church national office. Use the questions on the next page to prepare a separate data card for each newspaper you identify.

Include details of county or regional newspapers which are circulated within your town or territory, even if their office is technically outside of your church area.

Below is a sample, based on the make-believe town of Newtown, to show you what your completed card may look like.

Don't forget to note 'mechanical' data—i.e. What are the deadlines for copy? For photos? Are they different? Pictures usually have earlier deadlines than straight copy.

Make it a practice that if an editor tells you his deadline is one o'clock, you do not presume he will accept your copy up to that time. Rather you should allow him an extra day (for a weekly paper) and a couple of extra hours (for a daily).

Name:	Newtown Chronicle		
Address:	20/24 North Street, Newtown, NT1 1NC		
Telephone	0143-928-7654	Fax:	0143-928-7655
Circulation:	60,000	Area:	Newtown town and suburbs
Cost:	50p		
Published:	Weekly (Fridays)	Deadline:	Wednesday 5.00pm
Personnel:	Editor:		David Purkins
	News Editor		Sue McKenna
	Religious News Reporter		none
Editorial and news interest:	Primarily town, local and community news		
Disposition:	Open to local church contributions relevant to community.		

The kind of questions you should be asking are:

- What locally-published newspapers have a circulation in our town?
- Is there a daily newspaper? Is there more than one daily?
- Do they have more than one edition per day?
  Do they publish for daytime or evening circulation?
  What is their copy deadline?
- Are there weekly newspapers that have a circulation in our town?
- If so, what day do they publish? What is their copy deadline?
- Are there any Sunday papers published locally?
- Are there any ethnic newspapers published in our town?
- If so, what is their publication day, deadline, contact names and address, etc.?
- If there is a 'regional' or 'big city' newspaper with a circulation which includes our small town, does it have a correspondent local to us?
  Or will it accept local news direct?
- Are morning and evening newspapers under one joint management?
  If so, do they work co-operatively or competitively?
  Is material published in one likely to be used automatically in the other?
- Do weekly newspapers compete in any sense for news coverage with the dailies?
- Are several weekly papers combined under one management?
  Do they use material in common?
- Does our town have any free-circulation papers published and printed within it?
- Does the editor of any free paper(s) welcome local news?

You would apply a similar range of questions to local radio:

- Is there a 'Community' radio station in our town?
- Is there a BBC Local Radio station in our town or which reaches our town?
- Does that station have a religious programme producer?
- Is there a regular programme, such as a Sunday morning breakfast show, that carries religious items?
- Does the station broadcast regular services?
- Would they be interested in recording our church service for broadcast?

Assessing the actual responsiveness, and developing good relationships with your local media:

We've conceded that making first contact with professionals in the media can be daunting. But it is still not as bad as going to the dentist! A little homework and mental preparation will stand you in good stead. Much of it is down to knowing <u>what</u>, knowing <u>who</u>, and knowing <u>how</u>.

- You have got to know <u>what</u> really makes a good news story that is of interest to an editor.

- You need to know who to contact with that story so that it does not end up being ignored.

- You have got to learn how to contact them and how to present the item in a format they will appreciate.

We'll be dealing later with what makes a good story and how to present it successfully. For now we must concentrate on who to contact and how to contact them.

Buy all the local papers for a month, read them thoroughly so that you develop an instinct for the kind of news and style they carry. You will develop a 'feel' for the one most likely to print your church news items.

You will find that local papers vary just as national papers do. Some have a serious 'broadsheet' tone with a strong local-community spirit while others have a 'tabloid' tone with a penchant for the sensational—local crime, court reports, controversial local issues, dynamic or tragic human-interest stories.

This preliminary assessment is helpful so that you do not offer news items to media which would not be productively received. You may find a more ready response from the paper with the local-community orientation.

Personal contact is now vital. There simply is no substitute for meeting in person the editor or the journalist through whom most of your stories will be processed. Cultivate that relationship so that mutual confidence is possible.

Call at their office, with news release in hand. Ask to speak to the general editor or the news editor, introduce yourself and your role, and submit your news release to him or her. Specifically ask them what kind of stories they would welcome.

If you do not yet have a story to release, but want to establish contact in anticipation of the day when you do have a story, you can either:

* Call at their office with a church information pack, ask to meet the editor, and introduce yourself briefly in your role as church communication secretary. Enquire with whom you ought to make future contact, and how he/she likes to receive news items. Leave them your own name and number for future reference

* Telephone their office and ask if their paper has a 'Reader Panel' which you may join. Some newspapers have these as a way of involving their readership and keeping journalists in touch with their clientele.

Use a little tact and ingenuity when you introduce yourself. It is going to sit better if you introduce yourself with words like *'I've been appointed to help you cover news of my church'*, thereby suggesting you are there to volunteer help to him rather than that you are expecting him to serve the publicity ambitions of your church.

Once you have made contact with the right individual, you ought to systematically nurture it.

⇒ Send a Christmas card signed with personal greetings, to remind them who you are and of your interest in being of service.

⇒ Tip them off about other news stories that catch your attention, even those which have nothing to do with the church. This will confirm that you are interested in their general needs as a newspaper, and that you are not just looking for free publicity.

⇒ Find out the anniversary date of the paper and send a card with best wishes from the whole church family.

⇒ Send a 'Thank you' note at the end of the year—but not one which thanks them for 'all the publicity'. Just say 'Thank you for good coverage of the news relating to all the churches in our town'.

⇒ Get some of your church members involved with the media annual charity appeal.

⇒ Demonstrate that you regularly read their paper by writing to comment positively from time to time on items you have appreciated.

⇒ Whenever possible call personally to their office with your news item rather than posting it. This reinforces the 'personal touch' and the receptionist will get to know your smile!

In all your contact with the newspaper office, remember these ground rules:

- ***BE COMPETENT***. It is well-nigh impossible to compensate for poor material, poorly prepared, so do make sure you present items as 'professionally' as you can. Being competent also means that you will not make an obvious play for publicity as such. Submit newsworthy features, usable pictures, and observe deadlines. If you promise an 'exclusive', keep your word.

- ***BE COURTEOUS***. Respect the editor and never try to pressure him or her.

- ***BE THOUGHTFUL***.

1. By NOT calling on the editor when he is fighting his deadline.

2. By saying 'Thank you' and by sending an invitation to special seasonal church services such as the Christmas Carol Service.

3. By being friendly and brief in all your contacts.

- ***BE AVAILABLE***. Offer to respond punctually and personally to any enquiries the paper has at any time on stories that may effect the church.

Make sure your contact person knows that you are willing to put yourself out if necessary, and that you have contacts within the church network from whom you can get answers and official comments as may be helpful.

'Do not be nervous of journalists.
They are generally friendly,
eager to do a good job, and in most cases,
younger than you would expect.
If they see that you genuinely want to help,
you will be a welcome voice on the telephone
or caller to the office.'

Peter Crumpler in 'Keep In Touch'.

'Remember that journalists want to hear from you.
You will not be bothering them
or putting them out.
You may well have the news story
that is sufficiently "out of the ordinary"
to make the front page.'

Richard Thomas in
'An Introduction to Church Communication'.

Section Two: Setting Up Shop

Chapter Five:

Be Aware of the Hazards

Up to 50% of church correspondents feel the local media they have contacted were at best apathetic and at worst actively hostile. Many have had their fingers burned, and have subsequently vowed to keep well clear of all media, and certainly to withdraw from voluntary contact.

Perhaps we should be more intelligent about the factors that drive the media. They are businesses driven by commercial interests. Few have altruistic motivation. If truth were known, there is no high noble purpose, no compelling public interest that drives journalists to write and newspapers to publish. The bottom line is the need to make money. If it will sell newspapers, it will be utilized. If it won't, it will be ignored. There is nothing in their mandate which implies a duty to report favourably everything the church wishes, nor to turn a blind eye to unfavourable church news. Generally speaking, however, the local press extend even-handed treatment to the church as to other components of the community.

Some observers do detect a hostile stance in the national press to religious matters. Roy Greenslade, writing in PRESSWATCH: The Guardian (UK: 15/05/95), commented: **'In May 1995 there was a fascinating glimpse of the way in which the British press has not only marginalized religion and all its works, but boldly promulgates the view that it is now a potential danger to society. On Thursday (May 11) every paper carried the tragic story of Joy Senior, a woman who had knifed to death the three children she adored and then taken her own life. It was made infinitely more poignant by pictures of the smiling mother and children.**

'What had driven this poor woman to infanticide and suicide? Most papers were in no doubt. She was "Brainwashed by Bible cult", the Sun said.

'Most newspaper readers without any direct knowledge of the church have received a simple and sinister message: religion is bad for you. It warps the mind. It is just another drop of poison in the public imagination. We are becoming used to the idea that there are but small steps from church to sect to cult to occult, from respectable spiritual regeneration to malevolent mind-bending.'

What can we do to avoid 'bad press'? That is the theme of this chapter.

The national dailies are published in two formats—the broadsheet or the tabloid. For some reason there is often a relationship between the physical shape of the paper and the editorial approach. Broadsheet papers *tend* to be the more serious, the more fair-minded, and the more thorough and considerate of the whole story. Tabloid papers *tend* to be sensationalist, melodramatic, with a reputation for scant regard for damage to the subject unless it suits them.

The redeeming factor for local church communication secretaries is that most local and regional newspapers do have a 'broadsheet' mentality. They are disposed toward fostering the community spirit because it is in their interests to do so.

But even with them, there are hazards that an unprepared PR secretary can walk into which we will do well to note. Forewarned is forearmed. If the church communication secretary is aware of the potential hazards, there is no reason at all not to retain the initiative and make voluntary approaches to the local media. In most cases this will not be abused.

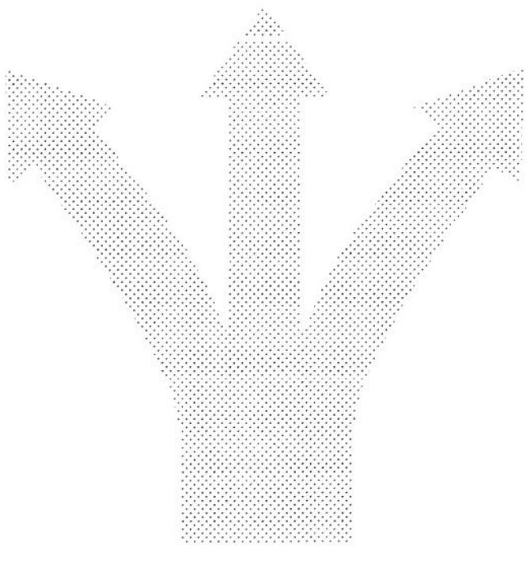

Simple ignorance may lead to inadvertent misrepresentation.

If the journalist does not have the correct information immediately to hand and does not know whom to contact in order to gain that information, he will use whatever is to hand that he believes is correct.

In most cases you would find little or no current data about your church on file at the local paper. The chances are there is no listing for your church in the telephone directory, and no indication of how to contact your minister—even if they know who he is. If that is true, we have no one to blame but ourselves. Who is going to provide current data about your church if you do not?

The journalist will therefore have to resort to what is readily to hand. He will look to see what an encyclopaedia or the Internet has on record, which may or may not prove to be as accurate or objective as you might prefer.

There is a simple remedy—we *must* ensure that editors and reporters have current fact sheets about the church, including updated names and phone numbers of strategic persons.

Occasionally a reporter will turn out to be unscrupulous.

Don't be lulled into a false sense of security. Occasionally a reporter will appear to be warm, understanding and compassionate during the interview but hostile or insensitive in print. He may get you to share information or a photograph which is then used in a way you regret.

Unfortunately that is the name of the game for some. They will try anything to get the edge on a competitor. They have little regard for the impact on their 'victim'.

Unless you know the reporter from past experience, be prepared for such abuse. Be on your guard and do not allow yourself to be lured into a false sense of confidentiality. You will have to assume that an underlying disposition to exploit *may* exist.

Remind yourself that as you build bridges with the newspaper or journalist, these circumstances may be avoided. You will learn who is trustworthy and can be relied upon to respect the sensitivities of the church. They will honour you and what you represent because of the kind of people they know comprise the church.

Because every media company has commercial motivation, it may network or franchise your statement nationally or internationally.

In our day of rapid electronic communication, it is possible for a newspaper to circulate stories, pictures, interviews and official comments around the world in moments. They do this because they make money from doing so.

This means it is potentially hazardous to make an indiscreet or undiplomatic comment on any sensitive issue or news item. An unguarded word, even one expressed casually, may be quoted and printed across the nation within hours.

The remedy is to determine not to make any unguarded statement on a subject which is remotely likely to have an interest to the media beyond the strictly local arena. It is best to refer journalists to your national or regional communication director for an official statement.

They will press you because quotes make good news copy. In this case, avoid any off-the-cuff comment. Prepare a written statement, which is carefully and prayerfully put together in counsel with the pastor and/or national church communication director, and issue only that printed statement with no further verbal comment at all.

Refusing to make any statement or comment can back-fire.

It is never good to refuse to make any comment at all, because the media are likely to put their own interpretation on your silence. It is better to say *'I am unable to make an immediate comment, but we will issue a formal statement as soon as I have consulted with my colleagues.'*

If you follow this approach, you must also be mindful of media deadlines. Your priority must be to get a statement into the *first* published report of the story because it is nearly impossible to repair damage done by that first report if it is wrong. Other papers will pick up that first report and use it as the basis for their own. Therefore it is important to explain your viewpoint or give the church's version of events when <u>first</u> approached by the media. Any delay at all must be *very* brief. The journalist wants a scoop, and has a deadline to meet so he will not wait hours for a formal comment.

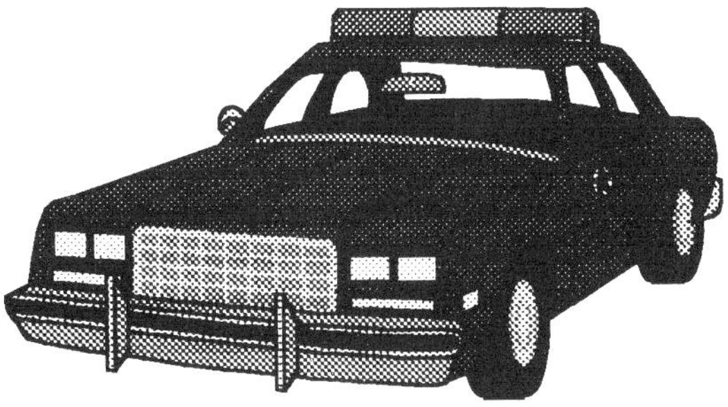

The media revel in 'fallen priest' or 'dotty vicar' stories.

The media bosses know that there is a public appetite for gossip. Stories of moral lapses in high places appeal to Joe and Josephine Public. In an inverted way, these stories help people to feel good about themselves.

Stories of moral lapses in church life or leadership create hazards for the church. It may then fall to the communication secretary to respond. There are simple rules which may alleviate some of the worst repercussions:

- Do not deny the facts.

- Do not refuse to co-operate with the press. But ask for time to check the facts before you make any comment.

- Do not volunteer additional information, names, addresses, phone numbers or photos.

- Do not make comment on anything about which you are not fully informed. Make certain anything you do say is accurate.

- Never say 'Yes' to words fed to you by a reporter. Anything you say may be reported as a quote. Limit the risk by issuing a brief but helpful prepared statement.

- Remember the theological framework within which your church functions, and never compromise it.

- Be guided by the old adage, 'If you cannot speak well of a person, say nothing about them at all.' Our best response is one of damage limitation by emphasizing all that is still good and honourable.

The media may accentuate the 'cult' or 'sect' tag.

Elements of a story may be exploited to play on the fears and anger of the public. By association with the 'cult' or 'sect' tag, an innocent church may be subjected to devastating speculation and suspicion. Sensationalism sells papers.

<u>The remedy is found in anticipation rather than in complacency. It is in attempting prevention rather than in attempting a cure.</u>

If local journalists know your church because they know you, and they know it to be composed of reasonable people of integrity who hold to sound, long-established Biblical teaching, the chances are these journalists will contact you if a sensational story arises which involves your church. They will give you a chance to contribute, react or correct the misinformation.

Your objective must always be to add positive input to the story *before its first publication* rather than have a knee-jerk reaction once the story is broadcast. If the local editor or reporter knows that you are always ready to provide a response or track down an official statement, they are likely to honour that by knocking at your door. Such preventative work is worth a thousand column inches of forlorn remedial work.

The media are not reluctant to feature deviations from the orthodox faith or standards of the church.

One bishop is reported as denying the basic tenets of Christianity; another is reported as having been convicted of gross indecency; another is reported as delivering a lecture that excuses adultery on the grounds that 'God gave us our genes'. The press love it, and feature it front-page. No sinister conspiracy is underway. It is simply a fact that contentious issues sell papers, and the press are in the business of selling papers.

We have to regret that Christians and church leaders do still make mistakes. We have to pray for integrity and honour among Christian leaders. Society is going to cast stones whether it is 'without sin' or not. One old Christian used to say that 'People who live in glass-houses should undress in the dark', and perhaps there is something in that!

There is hazard attached to maintaining any standard of the church which society would like to mock but sometimes this hazard can be turned to advantage. When the pastor makes a statement approving Sunday trading, it appears to go against orthodoxy, so use it to advantage to gain media interest!

If it all goes horribly wrong, and the tabloids splash the most dreadful reportage of news affecting your church, refer to Chapter 14 for further advice.

<u>Summary:</u>

Build positive contact with local media because prevention is easier to effect than cure.

Place positive data with the local media because it is vital it has accurate, current statistics and contact names on file.

Displace the 'isolationist oddity' perception because so long as the media perceive the church as a group who keep themselves much to themselves and have some odd notions about life and morality, it will generalize about it. □□

Section Two: Setting Up Shop

Chapter Six:

Understanding What Constitutes 'News'

Peter Crumpler quotes an intriguing story. A church publicity officer was challenging the editor of his local newspaper, 'What do we have to do to get more coverage in your newspaper?' That night their church was burnt down by vandals, and the story hit the headlines!*

No one would have wished for such a dramatic route to the front page, and of course there was no connection between the two events, but the incident does illustrate the problem the local communication secretary may have in getting anything printed by the local press. What happens behind closed church doors has little relevance to the editor because it is inconsequential to his reader. He could well be interested, however, by something that impacts upon his readership community!

The successful communication secretary is one who develops a 'nose' for what is or is not newsworthy. That means looking at the church from the outside, and thinking from a 'them and us' perspective, asking 'If I was a typical member of this community who seldom darkened the doors of a church, what would entice me to read about it?' Crack that, and you are well on your way.

Journalists, as we have noted, have an unhappy knack of hitting that particular bull's-eye quite regularly. They have a nose for what will trigger public interest in church news. Sadly that is often the 'bad news' so far as the church sees it, and our objective is to counter that as much as possible with positive images.

It is easy to think with despair: 'There's <u>nothing</u> happening in my church that would interest the press.' For some the opposite temptation exists—wistfully thinking that '<u>Everything</u> happening in my church merits press coverage'. Between those two extremes lies the truth, for from time to time there will be items that hold a public interest which are also positive from the church perspective. But how can we identify them? That's our next task.

(Peter Crumpler: 'Keep In Touch' p.91)*

We are going to attempt this task in what may seem to be a back-to-front way—we will start with a practical exercise and then talk theory afterwards! That way the theory may make sense more quickly.

Evaluate what constitutes church-oriented 'news' that catches the eye of the editor, by researching his papers over the past month or so.

Phone your local newspaper or library to see whether they provide access to back-numbers of their paper. Make arrangements to visit them for a complete morning or afternoon, and be prepared to commit yourself wholeheartedly to this project. Select a period of at least one month (preferably longer), and scan through every edition published during that time. You will soon learn which sections of the paper to dismiss without scrutiny because they carry sport or advertising.

Look out for any story or picture that had a church or religious connection. If it is possible, get a photocopy of each example you find, so that you can create an archive file, which you can then take home to evaluate at your leisure. Otherwise take a notepad with you and do an on-the-spot analysis of each sample.

This will cntail noting the date of publication, the church concerned, and the interest-factor of the storyline, trying to pinpoint what it was that caught the eye of the editor and caused him to publish the item.

When you have finished this project, write down in a sentence or two what you assess the editorial policy of that paper to be with regard to church or religious news: *'This paper seems to recognise and accept the newsworthiness of religious or church-oriented items when they . . ?* (Fill in the blank according to what you find, such as 'when they are controversial', or 'when they are local human-interest stories', or 'when they were timely and were reported promptly', and so on).

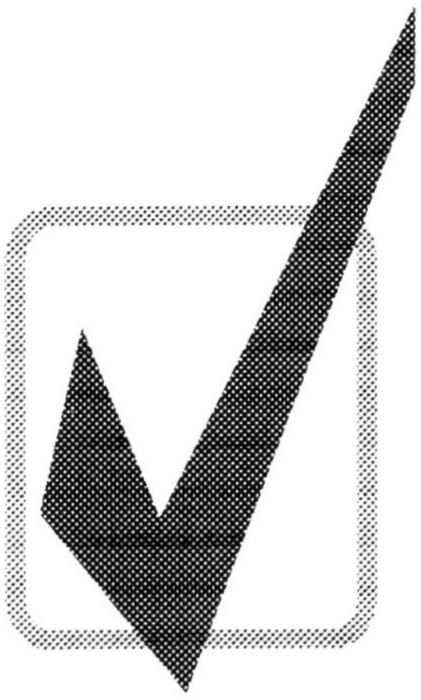

It really does not make much sense to proceed further until you can honestly put a 'tick' in the box to say *'Mission Accomplished'*. It is going to take some effort on your part to get to the place where you have an initial comprehension of what your editor smiles on, and there is no satisfactory alternative than to spend the necessary time to get it done by hard graft.

Of course, if you already take that paper in your home and have the back issues, you can do all your research in your own favourite chair!

With that experience under your belt, this is the point at which you can usefully look at the theory to see if what you have found in reality, comes close to what the textbooks suggest.

Acknowledge what does not qualify as 'news' in the local editor's mind.

Some church activity and information is of limited public interest because it would have to be defined as ***'domestic'***—having merely an 'internal' purpose, focus, objective or relevance. Some other church activity and information has wider public interest because it may justifiably be classified as ***'community'***—having some 'external' purpose, focus, objective or relevance. It is essential to learn to differentiate between the two!

The motivation of the church may well be Jesus' observation in Mark 13:10 that the *'gospel must first be preached to all nations'*. The 'bottom line' of our agenda could be Jesus' commission in Mark 16:15 to *'Go into all the world, and preach the gospel'*. However, these factors do not register on the agenda of the secular media, nor very much in the minds of their readers. We have to learn to acknowledge that our motivation and our agenda is ***'domestic'*** and often does not qualify as 'news' in the eyes of the press. Generally speaking, the papers want *'news, not the Gospel'!*

You will find during the research outlined in section 1 above, that Editors tend *not* to print 'preachy' church items. Perhaps there was a time and place where a newspaper published reports about details of church services and sermon content. You may even have seen items that reported which hymns the congregation sang! But you must not be surprised if your editor never publishes that kind of item if that is all you ever give him.

Nor will he receive as 'news' what in reality is an attempt to get free publicity for a 'domestic' event. If you want to promote an evangelistic meeting (which *would* be seen most definitely as 'domestic' by an editor), you must buy display advertising space, and not expect the editor to provide free publicity in his news columns where every inch is precious.

Anything that amounts to church propaganda, denominational posturing or doctrinal argument is also likely to be received as 'domestic'. The editor is not going to accept as news what amounts to a 'party political broadcast' on behalf of the (your church) party! He may print them under 'letters to the editor' but never as news.

'News' is something that the editor perceives to be of consequence to the community.

You can expect to find during your local research, that published stories are significant to the wider readership community and not just to a limited section of it. It will be of interest to the general readership and not just to church-goers.

Putting it bluntly, neither the public nor the press are interested in what seems to them to be the mundane private musings of a reclusive religious club. The media will usually *not* take the initiative to follow up 'internal' stories—*unless* they perceive those activities as sensational, clandestine or subversive, something that smacks of the 'cult' or 'sect' which would be controversial if published and therefore of wider interest.

BUT the public and the press will be interested by good human-interest stories that have local relevance and impact—stories that have an 'external' focus. So that is what we must seek to report.

We note again that the *raison d'etre* of the secular press has no overt religious component. Recognition of this fact of life may provide the opportunity for the church to radically rethink it's own *raison d'etre*, as suggested in the next chapter, and must stimulate the communication secretary to avoid annoying the local editor with items of a merely domestic nature.

We might summarize those items that *are* of interest by listing some catchy one-liners that seek to encapsulate a definition of 'news'. Compare and contrast them with your own research findings:

- News is both local **and** relevant.
- News is about *people*.
- News reports what is controversial, provocative.
- News is about challenges to authority.
- News is about extraordinary things being done by ordinary people, or ordinary things being done by extraordinary people.
- News is what some people wish had remained in the closet.
- News is what gets talked about over a pint.
- News is about changes—new staff, buildings, locations, missionary departures.
- News is about regular things—anniversaries and annual events.
- News is about new projects.
- News is about change, and yet is about regularity; about surprise and yet about confirmation; about conflict and yet about victory; about prediction of future events and yet about reminiscence of the past.

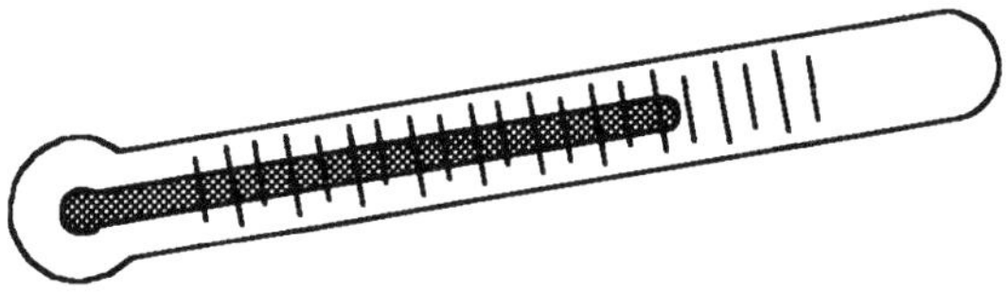

Developing a 'News-Value' gauge.

As you begin to sniff out stories in your local church, it is helpful to develop a 'News-Value' gauge.

There are five elements which tend to make a story 'newsworthy':

Human interest,
Prominence,
Consequence,
Timeliness,
Proximity.

As a fairly rough-and-ready guide to the value of a particular item, you should assess each story by asking whether it has *a minimum of three* of those elements.

Human interest: Your most captivating news stories or features are going to be human-interest stories—items which cause the reader to feel pleasure, pity, sympathy, delight, admiration or respect. They will be stories with which the reader can personally identify in some way because they touch the heart.

Prominence: When the people in your story or feature are prominent by virtue of their official position or their public reputation, your item is more newsworthy. A visiting national or world leader of your church holds an interest to your local media even if people in your town do not know him. A visiting well-known personality such as a Christian athlete or entertainer, has the same value.

Consequence: The event you are reporting needs to affect people in your town, or your community, or your church members in that community. It must have 'external' interest or impact.

Timeliness: Perhaps the most important element of all is that of timeliness. By definition, 'news' is something new that has just happened, and the report about it *must* reach the editor either before the event happens or on the very day it happens. For a daily paper, the event *must be* one taking place that day—not yesterday or earlier this week. For a weekly paper, the event *must be* one that has taken place during the week since their last publication date, and up-to-and-including the next publication date.

Proximity: To be of interest to the *local* media, the event you are reporting must be one that is happening or has happened 'here'—right in your town or community.

If you can report stories or features that incorporate all five elements on the ***'Profile of Newsworthiness'*** gauge, then you should be laughing all the way to the editor's office. But if you cannot see a minimum of three of those elements, then you should probably save his time and your own by not proceeding with it.

In a later chapter we will be looking at specific ideas and news opportunities that may arise in the local church.□□

Section Three: News Stream

Chapter Seven:

News Opportunities in the Local Church.

If you've taken Section Two on board, then you've made the first steps toward setting up shop as communication secretary for your local church. There's a way to go yet, but at least you are beginning to come to terms with the task and your approach to it.

For example,

- *You have your 'office' established with necessary hardware and software, and you have your 'modus operandi' mentally mapped out.*
- *You have assessed your local media and you know who to approach. Hopefully you have already made personal contact with them or will do so very shortly.*
- *From your careful analysis of published church items in the local press, you have some comprehension of what constitutes 'news' that is likely to be well received by your editor(s).*
- *You have a mental picture of the* ***'Profile of Newsworthiness'****,*
- *And you have determined how your congregation sees itself and how it wishes to interface with its community and the media.*
- *You have an agreed 'mission statement' which the church have jointly assembled.*

But now you are beginning to ask 'How can I marry all these factors together and turn theory into practice? Where can I see my first news release coming from? How can I keep the ball rolling once started?' It's time to look at news opportunities that may occur in your church, and at how to 'make' some news if the present situation looks a bit barren.

News opportunities involving PEOPLE:

Church is all about people. That should give us a head-start with the media bosses, because they know their public like reading about people. The most enticing stories are those with human interest. People like to see themselves in print, or to have the low-down on somebody they know from along the street.

The effective communication secretary homes in on 'people stories', which will probably fall into one of four categories:

- The ministry, staff and leaders;
- The church family and its programme;
- The members and children as individuals;
- Church and society 'personalities'.

The kinds of thing that may suggest a story are:

- Staff and ministry changes:

Whenever an existing minister is moving away or retiring, there is a news opportunity. Whenever a new minister arrives, there is another news opportunity.

Changeover of local leaders can provide a story, perhaps linked with a deliberately tongue-in-cheek 'slug-line' such as ***'Church Leaders Dismissed!'*** followed with a report that says:

'It's all-change at First Church, Newtown. Every single local leader has been changed for the New Year at the Long Street Church. "But there's no scandal, and no disgrace!" Pastor Pete Durrant explained. "We are a very active church, and we change our leaders round every year," he said.' Submit a photo of the retiring elder shaking hands with the incoming elder, with smiles all round.

- Visits & Departures:

Youth volunteers leaving for overseas projects; local-born people leaving for any out-of-the-ordinary overseas post—including departing or returning missionaries or aid workers; state or church dignitaries visiting or departing; unusual holidays with a purpose (such as building a clinic in a developing country)—all these and more suggest news opportunities.

Perhaps a church member is obliged to seek work overseas because of unemployment at home. Whether it's an engineer departing for work in the Gulf States, a computer programmer leaving for Papua New Guinea, or graduate chiropractic going to teach English in China for a year, they can be pictured receiving a farewell gift from the church, under a catchy title.

For example, when one church member had to seek work abroad, a news release could have been issued: ***Unemployed Newtown man leaves family for Kuwait.'*** A photo of the church presentation could have been included, with the caption: *'Out-of-work Newtown man Jerry Hale has had to resort to extreme measures to support his family. A skilled aircraft engineer, he departs Monday June 1 for Kuwait where he will train local apprentices. Mr Hale is pictured receiving five cases of non-alcoholic wine from his friends at First Church, Long Street. Like the Muslims of Kuwait, First Church members are teetotal.'*

- Individual achievement or involvement:

Unusual milestones, achievements or involvement of your members has news interest. For example, driving a truck of relief aid; reaching a significant marriage anniversary; completing an unusually long service for one company; achieving academic success against odds such as a handicap; members with unusual hobbies; reunion of long-separated family; participation in international youth project; unusual holidays with a humanitarian purpose; senior citizens holiday with a difference; imaginative Community projects; out-of-the-ordinary Pathfinder events; and so on. There always needs to be a link to a local individual or family.

News opportunities involving SPECIAL EVENTS:

Church is also about special events which might include:

◊ Regular 'diary' events such as: landmark denominational anniversary celebrations; local church organisation anniversaries; new church building ground-breaking ceremony.

◊ Very special events which may become regular diary anniversaries: A new church building project provides a number of news opportunities at different stages: land purchase, planning approval, fund-raising efforts, ground breaking, presentation of keys, inauguration or dedication, official opening by mayor.

◊ Irregular, one-off events such as: concerts; festivals; pilgrimages; lecture series; overnight or unusual youth events; launch of community club for senior citizens; inter-city youth days; health / exercise / family seminars; international camporees or congresses; children taking the church service or preaching the sermon; holiday Bible school; or a baptism in a local river.

When a significant fund raising project has been completed, it is often possible to get the bank to provide a large-format presentation cheque. Good PR can be achieved with a formal presentation to the beneficiary.

News opportunities involving SPECIAL PROJECTS:

Because readers like human interest stories, they like reading about humanitarian or community projects. A dynamic congregation is likely to have some of the following occurring from the church base: Special Relief Aid collections or deliveries; fund raising for well known charities; sponsored events for local funds or projects; soup kitchen at the church; soup run for the homeless.

News opportunities from the SERMON:

Most newspapers will not use sermon reports, except those that are on provocative issues, those that relate to current affairs, or those from high profile services or funerals. A reading of your own local papers will clarify the potential in your case.

If you can see the possibility of submitting a sermon report, make sure it is timely and relevant to your community. No sermon report will be printed unless it says something that readers can apply to their own world and their own current needs or concerns. The communication secretary may occasionally need to be bold and suggest directly to the minister that he/she might address a subject that does touch on today's need as felt in that community.

You might try thc following steps and technique:

1. Contact the speaker ahead of time to let him/her know your intention to try a sermon report, and ask whether their subject tackles a current issue. If so, ask for some germane quotable quotes.

2. Extract a single punchy topic sentence that will catch the eye of the editor or reader—such as *'Pastor preaches in favour of Sunday Trading!'* Use this as the 'slugline' and as the opening line in your first paragraph, immediately followed by the identification of the speaker.

3. In succeeding paragraphs, state the occasion of the sermon. Use further statements from the speaker making direct quotes. All quotes MUST be accurate and attributed to the speaker. Never attribute something to him which the speaker did not actually say.

4. Avoid descriptive words which give the impression the preacher was ranting like an extremist. Seek to bring out some vital point which touches on essential Christian beliefs.

5. Keep it brief. The report need not be long. It does require to be pithy, provocative, and locally relevant—scratching where the public already itch, or creating a new itch in their minds which they will feel to be healthy and helpful.

News opportunities that are MADE:

It is entirely legitimate to 'make' news. 'Making' news simply means taking the initiative to originate an event or story that will interest the media. It needs to be done well so that it does not attract the 'publicity stunt' tag, but creative lateral thinking is warranted and acceptable.

In Denmark a few years ago, Pathfinders were fund-raising for a mission project in Pakistan. Their leaders hit on the idea of accumulating as many 5p coins as possible. This was one of their lowest-denomination coins and had the advantage of a hole through the middle. Collecting them became infectious among the young people, to the point that banks were running short.

Eventually the Pathfinders gathered at one market square and strung their coins end-to-end, making a line dozens of metres long which took several strong youth to carry and deposit in the nearby bank. It attracted huge interest and was widely reported in the national media. That is what 'making' news is all about—seeing an opportunity to capitalize on a simple idea to win media coverage.

The ingenuity of the communication secretary now comes into play. Here's what to do:

* Review your local papers again to spot stories that were 'made' rather than just happened. You will find many of them.

* Take samples of these stories to each of the leaders of the departments in your church—children, Scouts or Pathfinders, community services, etc., and ask them to provide you with at least one 'happening' that you may jointly 'make' into a newsworthy event.

* For example, when the deacons are preparing to redecorate the youth hall, suggest they choose a retired craftsman painter/decorator and have him 'apprentice' the teenagers for the week, and train them how to paint. Occasionally papers like these 'homely' style of items submitted with a warm friendly photo which shows that the generation gap does not always dominate life for the teenager.

* If your local leaders cannot think of anything in their programme from which you can 'make' a story, give them the following list to provoke their thinking.

⇒ **Make a survey and render a report.** Take some members with clipboards and survey pads, and spend a couple of hours on your high street. All kinds of subjects are suitable: 'Is Christmas too commercialized?'; 'Do you approve of Sunday trading?'; 'Should religious programmes be dropped from TV?'; 'Is there too much religion in Easter television?' Collate the findings, and write up a report for the local press.

'Four out of five Brentford and Chiswick shoppers agree that Christmas is too commercialised. This week, one of Chiswick's newest churches surveyed shoppers to find out if we have lost sight of the real meaning of Christmas.'

Quoted by Peter Crumpler in his book **Keep In Touch**, this was the opening paragraph in an article which went on to provide comment from the survey organizer.

⇒ **Embellish an event.** Like the Danish Pathfinder fund raising event, use imagination to amplify or elaborate the news potential of what may otherwise be mundane or quickly forgotten. A mass balloon-release may be too common nowadays, but a church where everybody, from infant to nonagenarian wields a spade, paintbrush or broom to help clear the church premises *may* just catch the eye.

⇒ **Create or conduct a special event.** Run a Gospel Music Festival for inner-city youth, or an 'Oldest/Smallest Bible Contest'. Present a Christmas tableau. Enter a float in the local carnival.

⇒ **Other suggestions include:**

◊ Give an award. Contact your national church office for award medallions such as for Service in the Community.

◊ Relate your church to a well-known personality. Invite a high-profile Christian athlete to address your youth on the drugs-in-sport issue.

◊ Make a charge. Society is concerned about the detrimental effect of too much sex and violence on TV. Some are concerned about the breakdown of the family unit; others about the impact of Sunday trading; others about the exposure of children to alcohol-promotional environments. Become known as builders of society by making appropriate charges about injurious developments in our culture.

◊ Render a public service. Provide a day nursery for kids, or a 'drop-in' club for OAPs. Stage a work bee for an aged person, or organise your teenagers to clear rubbish in a community play area.

Summary:

It may sound too good to be true. It may seem only remotely possible from your past experience. But if the stance of your congregation is toward its community rather than in retreat from it, there will be considerable potential for news items.

Sometimes these will be attached directly to the church as such, and other times they will be incidentally attached to the church by reference to a member. Sometimes they will relate to events that just 'happen' and at other times they will be 'made' to happen. But the opportunities do exist. We just need to market them. □□

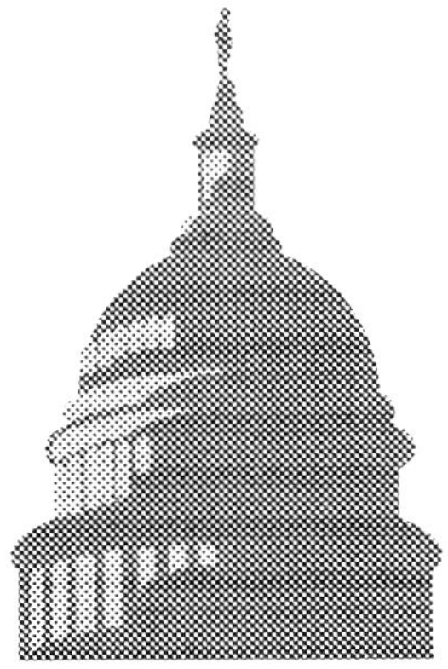

Section Three: News Stream

Chapter Eight:

The All-important 'News Release'

The most effective way of bringing news items to the attention of the media is by the **'News Release'**. *In laymen's language this is a brief report to the newspaper which 'waves a flag' to attract attention to your story. It is a simple, lucid and logical presentation of information written to include every essential detail about What? Where? When? Why? the event is happening, and Who? it involves and How? it involves them. It must be presented so that a journalist can make a fairly instant decision about how to proceed with it. The news release is not intended, of itself, to be a major literary work, so do not get carried away.*

Contact with the newspaper staff will provide opportunity to ask how they like releases to be presented—whether they prefer them to be more or less ready-to-print without much further work, or a skeleton which they will 'fill out' themselves by interview or by attending with a reporter and cameraman. You may find their response will vary from story to story. As your contact with the press is extended, so your confidence will grow and you will learn just how to submit material with success.

Since you want to be as effective as possible, it will pay dividends to make yourself aware of the standards they typically work to. This chapter is all about trying to meet those standards.

Newspapers are staffed by professional journalists for whose attention there is fierce competition. They are receiving news releases from a host of other commercial media sources. They are courted by freelance news agencies trying to earn a living by selling them stories and leads. They are wooed by PR professionals engaged by local and national commercial and political entities. And yet they have an ear for ordinary Mr or Mrs Joe Public.

To have a realistic chance of attracting their attention, however, we must try to present our material in as professional and helpful a way as possible. We shall need to look closely at the standards they expect, in relation to *Format*, *Accuracy*, *Presentation*, *and Support*.

Media expectations relating to the FORMAT of your news release.

Use standard A4 typing paper for all news releases you submit and for all your regular correspondence with the media. Type releases using only a single side of the paper, double spaced between lines, and allowing at least a 2.5cm (1") margin on both sides. Except for 'Letters to the Editor', handwritten submissions are likely to be discarded. The standard expectation is for typed or word-processed news releases.

Identify yourself boldly leaving no chance for confusion. It is worth the investment of going along to your local instant printers and having them design and print a special 'Press Release' sheet. They will usually have some samples from which you can select. A sample Press Release is shown later in this chapter, which may provide a specimen for news release stationery.

use of a tinted paper may help the journalist find your item in a mixed pile. Perhaps the national office of your church will be able to supply you with its standard news-release stationery onto which you can custom-print local identification details.

Normal letterheads are often NOT suitable for news releases because they may contain name and address details which do not apply. Never use standard stationery which bears contact data for anyone not directly involved with this specific release. The only phone numbers shown on the release should be of those who know about the subject of the news release.

However, it is good if your church can afford a localised letterhead which incorporates the national logo of your church. This helps you to establish a readily-recognised corporate identity which will be helpful in the general purposes of good PR.

You may be able to place a small order for about 100 copies rather than for a full ream. Remember that

Anchor the date and purpose of your news release, by stating at the head of the paper the date of issue, the purpose of issue, and the date for publication. Contact names and numbers are usually given at the foot of the release.

In most cases your item will be 'For Immediate Release', so you should indicate this at the head of the page, as shown on the Sample which follows. If the item is for future release, indicate this clearly 'For Release June 1', for example.

Occasionally an item will be 'embargoed' until a subsequent date, which should also be clearly stated. Embargoed stories will strictly not appear in print until the declared date, and it is taken that this date shall be mutually respected.

Embargoed releases allow for journalists to research stories in more detail so that they may be ready with all the information they require by the time the release date is reached. For example, a TV company may 'embargo' the results of a contest but recognise that the papers will want to publish the full story as promptly as possible once permitted. This system allows the necessary time to complete such preparations and still bring the story 'fresh' to the public, yet preserve the tension of the televised final. Such an item would be marked at the head: **EMBARGOED until 00.01am Monday May 1**, for example.

Leave space at the head of your copy for the editor's notes or comments. You can achieve this space by beginning your story not less than 8cms. (3") from the top of the sheet. You should also leave at least 4cms (1.5") clear at the foot of the page.

Do not divide a word between lines, and avoid dividing a paragraph between pages.

Make clear indication at the foot of the page whether this is the complete item by clearly typing 'MORE' or 'ENDS'. Alternately you may use the symbol ## or □□ to mark the end of an item.

Make clear identification at the head of the succeeding page(s) by listing your church name, the 'slug-line' of your item, the page number, and the total number of pages involved. For example type: 'Page 1 of 2'.

Be brief One page is all you should anticipate writing for a news release. Use two at the very most. If the paper wants more information, they will come after it.

Do not write more than one story on a page. If you have more than one item to report, issue a separate news release for each.

Do not write a headline for your item. This is the task of a sub-editor at the newspaper. Instead, write a 'slug-line'—a three or four word punchy statement that indicates the nature of the release.

Identify contact names and numbers at the foot of your release. If the paper wants to follow up your item, they will want ready access to contact persons. The foot of the release is the recognised location for this information.

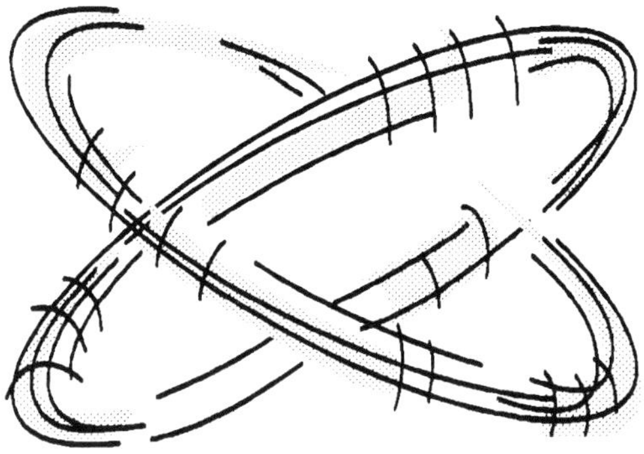

Post, fax or personally deliver your release in good time. If it is old, it just isn't news anymore.

Many have found that they can enhance the reception of their release by phoning the newspaper office before dispatching the copy. It is a good idea, and a simple technique to follow.

When your story is prepared, phone their office and ask to speak to the news desk or to a known reporter. Float the story with them, being sure to tell them What? When? Where? Why? Who? and How? If the journalist confirms interest, ask to whom you should address the release, and then make sure they get it that day.

This quick telephone call has the effect of alerting the reporter or editor to your release, so that when it arrives later that day they are already looking out for it. It sometimes pays to make a follow-up call to confirm that your item reached them as planned.

Media expectations relating to ACCURACY AND INCLUSIVE CONTENT.

A student wishing to sell-on some textbooks that he no longer had use for, placed an Ad. on the student notice-board: *'YOU NEED THESE BOOKS'*. He then catalogued the items, linking them to the courses for which they were mandatory. The list was accurate and the prices were right, but no one made any move to contact him.

Disappointed, he returned to his Ad. and underlined the words in red to emphasise *'YOU NEED THESE BOOKS!'*, but still no one came. Finally he went to remove the Ad., and found scrawled upon it, *'Yes, I know I need them, but who are you and where can I find you?'*

He had fallen into the most common trap of communication—he had failed to make sure he included the vital information summarised by the famous **five W's and the H**—Who is selling What, When, Where, Why, and How.

You have probably heard radio music-request programmes when the announcer has conveyed birthday greetings to 'Auntie Lily, with best wishes from all at No.155 Robin Hood Road—whoever they may be!'—because they failed to identify themselves.

The basic rule for communication secretaries in writing news releases must be that every release incorporates those essential six elements—***What? Who? Where? When? Why? and How?***

As Howard Weeks has written in his bench-mark work *'Breakthrough—A Public Relations Guidebook For Your Church'*:

'Who is being featured, speaking, leading out? What is being done, said, proposed, criticised, commended? When is it being presented, done or said? Where is the programme or speech being given? Why is it being done? Why is this a special occasion? Why is this being said? Why is this significant? How is the programme being carried out; how is it proposed that a problem be solved?'

Media professionals anticipate that a news release will include these vital details—the 'BIG SIX', as they have been called. Pick up a copy of your local paper and scrutinise the first paragraphs of each story on the front page. You may not find every detail in the opening sentence, but the paragraph will almost certainly incorporate every major fact. They are printed here because that may be all the reader will read.

The media professional will also anticipate that every detail will be accurate and complete. A good communication secretary makes accuracy a passion.

Be certain that names are stated in full, and accurately spelled. Be sure that titles, ranks, roles, qualifications and positions are exact.

Double-check for yourself, the accuracy of every name spelling, every date, time and place listed, and any comparative claim made within the article. By this we mean, if you want to report a gospel music festival as being 'the largest in Newtown this century', you must be certain that this comparative claim is accurate. Don't embarrass yourself or the church by making a claim that is not true.

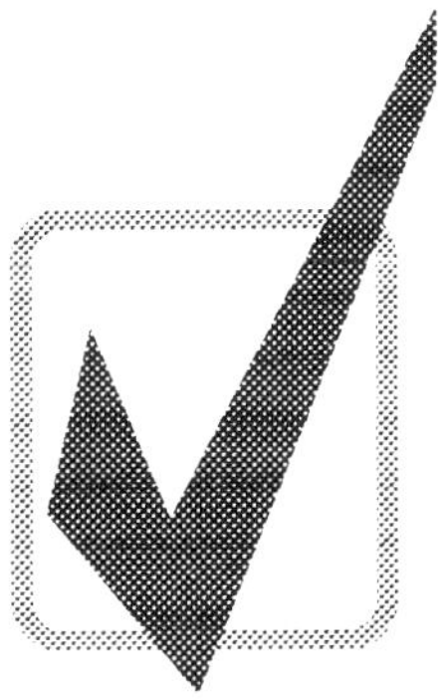

Avoid denominational or religious terms and expressions. Jargon jars! Avoid 'brother', 'sister', 'gospel', 'service', 'bless' (or 'blessing' and 'blessed'), 'Christ', 'redemption', 'atonement'.

Most journalists and readers do not know the difference between priests, pastors, vicars, or elders, so tell them. They will not be familiar with Bible or denominational names used for church departments—ask yourself for example, what relevance 'The Dorcas Society' would have to the average non-church reader.

Never use the abbreviation for your church name because it usually means nothing to the reader, or may be confused with some other entity.

Avoid flowery phrases or adjectives that are not purely factual. For instance, do not report a '*wonderful*' sermon or that '*glorious*' old hymn. Trying to influence your reader's opinion by expressing your own in this way is called **editorialising** and it is not acceptable practice.

Media expectations relating to the <u>PRESENTATION</u> of your news release.

You have two objectives in submitting a news release—initially you want to succeed in winning the editor's attention and get published, and ultimately you want to succeed in winning the reader's attention and get read. We have previously discussed what attracts an editor in terms of content (human interest stories related to his community readers). Now we must look at writing and presentation style which will achieve those two objectives.

Imagine yourself as a motorist trying to flag down passing drivers on a busy trunk road. They are all steaming by, totally preoccupied with keeping ahead of everybody else. So if you are going to succeed, you have to have a significant means of flagging them down safely.

You are not going to 'stop' the editor or his reader unless you hit them with the most interesting features right at the beginning in the opening words. You are not Agatha Christie trying to tease your reader to the very end. Newspaper readers should be looked on as 'readers on the run'. So if your story is going to get across, it must make impact in the first couple of seconds.

Your opening paragraph is called the ***'lead'*** and should contain as many of the 'BIG SIX' as possible. So ask yourself:

What points of public interest can I make most of in this story?

What is it that makes <u>this</u> a news story above the commonplace?

How can I write a lead paragraph to contain the most interest-grabbing feature within the first words of my opening sentence?

How can I incorporate the What? Who? When? Where? Why? and How?

There is another practical reason for including the most significant elements of your story high up in your release. An editor looking to crop a story short is inclined to edit out the later paragraphs. If the significant elements are retained for those closing paragraphs, they may well be lost. So view your release as an inverted triangle tapering off to a point. Since it is the taper that may succumb to the editor's red pen, make sure your vital information is all included at the head, not the tail.

The lead paragraph should be a concise summary of the whole story, but it's not good to artificially cram it with detail. Better to carry supporting elements over to a second paragraph.

Step One, therefore, is to arrange your facts so that the most exciting are ranked highest.

Step Two is to write your lead, jumping right into your story as quickly yet briefly as possible. Use short sentences and short paragraphs. You can test your lead by seeing if it is possible to draft a headline using only this as your source. Your editor is likely to write his headline from your lead, so if you cannot see the headline within it, neither will he!

Step Three is to write your subsequent paragraphs. These will build on your lead, perhaps explaining it in more detail and completing the story. Keep each paragraph crisp and punchy. Check your local paper to see how this works for other news items.

Use strong active verbs whenever possible because that makes for more dynamic reading. But let your style be relaxed and realistic. Ensure you answer any question posed by your opening paragraph, and do not arouse curiosity that your story will not satisfy.

Attribute statements to significant people in the story. Direct quotes are good because they give life. They are used in nearly every news story—check your own paper to see this.

It is perfectly all right to use 'said' frequently. Indeed, an obvious attempt to avoid repeating 'said' can become annoying.

Quotes are usually 'attributed' to an authoritative person involved in the story, or classified as 'non-attributable' when a spokesperson makes a statement on behalf of the organisation but themselves remain anonymous. For example:

- Mrs Joyce Claridge, Chair of the Newtown Temperance Federation, said 'We vigorously oppose the application to extend opening hours for licensed premises in the town centre.'

Or non-attributably:

- 'We know a lot of our customers want fewer restrictions to having a quiet pint when they feel like it,' a spokesman for the Newtown Brewery said.

Media expectations relating to <u>SUPPORT</u> of your news release.

Your purpose in 'waving a flag' at the editor is that he will want to take up the story. You hope this will mean he will dispatch a reporter and/or photographer to follow it up. This being your intention, you must be available and have access to support material as appropriate.

You will provide names and phone numbers for important contact persons by including them at the foot of your news release. You will then ensure that these people are accessible. You may sometimes also need to prepare a briefing pack or fact sheet which will provide background information which could be used in addition to the simple news release.

The fact sheet helps your editor grasp wider dimensions of a story, see greater possibilities for the story, or serve as information which will be placed on file for future reference.

Generally the news release is sufficient, but occasionally something larger comes into the frame—as in the CARE item used as a model at the end of this chapter. The editor will know about establishments such as International Red Cross, but not necessarily about less widely known groups. In such cases, your fact sheet would include:

- The 5 W's and H in detail.
- Prominent persons involved.
- Extent of impact of the event or organisation.
- Unusual features of the event or organisation.
- Links with church world work or with other organisations.
- Picture possibilities suggested.

Sometimes you can present a fact sheet in a question-and-answer style. In this case you anticipate the various questions a journalist may ask and list them with the answers a church representative would give along with other relevant facts and figures. □□

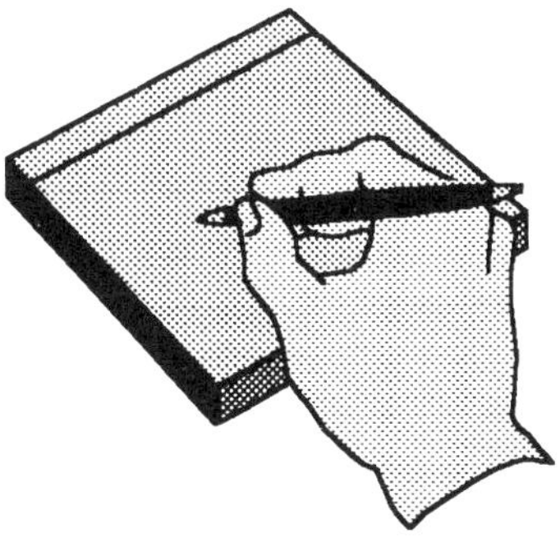

First Church
15 Long Street, Newtown

NEWS RELEASE

For the attention of the Editor, Newtown Gazette
1 May 1995
For immediate release.

Escape from Sarajevo

Newtown builder Jim Woods is relieved to be home today after being held hostage in Sarajevo for three weeks. He drove much-needed aid to the city as part of relief convoy, and found his return route sealed off by Serb militia.

First Church in Long Street, Newtown, sponsored Jim and asked him to deliver to a **CARE** warehouse in the wore-torn Bosnian capital. "The mountain roads were treacherous," said Mr Woods, "And several times we were caught in sniper fire. My truck is riddled with shell holes," he said.

"It's good to have him home safe and sound," his wife Maureen said at their Chiltern Street home. "When the Serbs closed the airport, we thought he might get caught up in the war," she said.

CARE, the **C**hristian **A**ssociation for **R**elief in **E**mergency, is an international non-denominational affiliation of Christian organisations in Europe distributing food and relief world-wide.

Jim and Maureen will be showing a video and talking about Jim's travels at a special open meeting at 7.00pm Monday 10th May, at the Long Street Church.

ENDS.

Photo enclosed. Journalists and photographers welcome at May 10th meeting.
Immediate interviews available.
Further information:
Communication secretary: George Ryan Tel. 214365 (home) 224356 (work)
or minister: Pastor Don Peters Tel 216543

First Church
15 Long Street, Newtown

FACT SHEET
CARE = CHRISTIAN ASSOCIATION for RELIEF in EMERGENCY

For the attention of the Editor, Newtown Gazette
1 May 1995

What:

CARE is an international, non-denominational association of Christian Relief and Development organisations in Europe. From its origins in 1980 it has grown into a major charitable operation with an annual budget of millions of pounds. Every year governmental and non-governmental aid organisations in Europe, including the UK, channel benefit worth millions through CARE, for disaster relief and community development projects. It is ranked ninth largest international voluntary organisation in the world.

Where:

CARE-UK is co-ordinated from a national office at Beta Park, Oldtown. CARE-Europe is operated jointly from Paris and Budapest.

Why:

Evangelical Christians have always believed that spiritual and mental health on the one hand, and physical well-being on the other, are closely related. By co-ordinating their work through CARE small individual churches are able to participate in the operation of a network of relief and development projects, frequently in places where there is no other facility.

When:

CARE seeks to respond to crises caused by natural and conflict-born disasters, and to the on-going needs in developing communities.

How:

Work ranges from well-drilling to agricultural development, and providing temporary shelter, food and clothing in war-torn countries. Major projects have been successfully operated to Azerbaijan victims, to Somalia, Chile, and Peru. 12,000 tonnes of food and clothing has been sent to Bosnia during the recent civil war.

Who:

For CARE-Newtown, contact Pastor Don Peters on Newtown 216543
For CARE-UK, contact Pastor Douglas Arthur on 0115-000-0000

(This fact sheet covers an hypothetical organisation to demonstrate style, format and content).

Section Three: News Stream

Chapter Nine:

Interviews and Press Conferences

If your news release strikes a positive response with the editor, a journalist is likely to contact you to confirm details or to make sure they understand the story. He or she may ask follow-up questions with a view to developing an interesting individual angle on the story, or may need to identify a time and place for a photograph.

You can make good use of these conversations to learn more about how to write your next release. Perhaps the reporter is asking something that you should have included in the original release but failed to do so. Don't be offended, but do make note of the kind of detail that was missing and ensure this is included in your subsequent work.

When responding by phone in this impromptu way, always make sure you give accurate answers. You should learn to expect reporters to contact you, and to anticipate their questions by learning as much as possible first-hand about the subject during your earlier research. Find out at the same time whether the person who is the subject of your release would be willing to receive a phone call direct from the reporter. If you should find yourself unable to answer a specific question, offer to get back to the paper very promptly with an accurate answer. Better still, offer an interview opportunity. Do not be tempted to guess or prevaricate!

Providing interviews is one of the primary aims of submitting your news release. You want to bring your journalists and your church to meet each other, because that is the way people learn more objectively about you. Jim Woods, the hypothetical truck driver whose story was cited in the news release on page 47, is a good example of the kind of subject a newspaper editor may wish to have interviewed. He has an unusual but very topical experience that the paper will want to report immediately, but his story might also be developed by the journalist into a 'feature' (see Chapter 11). If you sense an interest, ask the reporter, 'Would you like to talk directly to the person concerned? If so I can give you a phone number or arrange a meeting.'

This chapter is intended to help you handle a press interview and in exceptional circumstances to organise a press conference.

Preparing and running the press interview.

When you wrote your news release, one of your objectives was to attract the editor's attention sufficiently to cause him to send a journalist to interview the subject. Therefore a lot of the research and preparation you did before you put pen to paper will remain useful during this follow-up by the reporter.

In anticipation that you will secure a press interview you should do a preliminary interview with the subject yourself. Not only will this provide you with the basic nuts-and-bolts of your story and fact sheet, but it will also be mutual preparation for the real thing.

When the press contact you to arrange an interview, you may feel you can leave it to the reporter to make arrangements himself, and in some circumstances this may be more convenient so that press deadlines can be met. In this case, if you have prior permission from the candidate you may provide the reporter with a phone number for direct contact.

But there are advantages to arranging the interview yourself and attending it in company with the candidate. You want to meet staff reporters as often as possible to build a helpful contact with them, so do not pass up these opportunities when they come.

Confirm with the candidate that he/she is available for interview at the arranged time and place. Adjust the meeting if necessary. Then be on hand yourself for the interview to make sure it comes off as scheduled. Above all, the reporter must not arrive and find no one there. You are responsible for making sure the candidate keeps the appointment.

Present the reporter with a copy of any printed release and then let them do the interviewing. You should not interrupt unless the interview is floundering and you can think of a way to pull it back on course. Your fact sheet should help the reporter ask the right questions. Towards the end of the interview he/she may ask you if anything has been overlooked.

Alert your subject that pictures will probably be taken, and ask them to bring along any objects that will enhance the relevance of the photos—in Jim Woods' case, for example, it would be well to have the photo session with his truck in the background to show the shell scars.

Remember you are always talking 'on the record' when with a reporter. Whatever you say may be picked up and used in his copy, so be careful about everything you say including 'tonguc-in-the-cheek' remarks.

If you want to speak 'off the record' you must make this clear to the journalist. He will know such comment is for his ears only and not for publication. It may sometimes help to clarify some background detail if you offer, *'Would it help if we spoke off the record for a moment?'*

Always check from time to time that you are still 'off the record', and confirm with the journalist when you are going back 'on record'. An 'off the record' briefing is helpful to a journalist who may not know about the inner workings and mysteries of your church. It helps in framing more informed questions to ask once back 'on record'.

Interviews should always be offered with some 'exclusive' element to them. In other words, even if more than one paper sends a reporter to an event at a given time and there is some 'general' period when they all share question and answers in a sort of 'mass interview', there should be opportunity to speak to each paper in isolation from the others. This will allow them to create their own angle on a story. For this reason there are occasions when reporters will not want their particular line of questioning to be overheard by rivals and part of the communication secretary's role will be to ensure privacy.

At the conclusion of the interview make sure the reporter has your phone number for any further help he may need.

Preparing and running the Press Conference.

A press conference differs from a press interview in that it is formally called at the initiative of the party making the news release. It is an organised and disciplined briefing that is carefully controlled by the first party or their agent. Sufficient notice is communicated to all relevant media companies so that they may attend if they wish.

Press Conferences are useful in a number of situations.

* It may be that the organisation needs to brief the media about a developing story. Perhaps one company is merging with another, and jointly they may wish to release an official statement.

* It may be about the launch of a significant statement or product. A motor company is launching a new model and wants the world to know about it.

* It may announce a major appointment and present the appointee to the public. United have signed a new player!

Press conferences provide a convenient opportunity for journalists to put direct questions to the candidate in company with their opposite numbers from other papers. The chance for individual interviews is not automatically provided.

Realistically a press conference is most unlikely to be necessary for a local church communication secretary. It would be unusual for something as significant as that to occur within a local church. If it does, it is also most likely that the matter would need to be handled by the regional or national PR officer for the denomination. But if it should occur, make arrangements as follows.

Whenever possible take into consideration the deadlines impinging upon the media. In cases when the press conference is a response to a crisis it may not be possible to set up the conference sufficiently in advance as to take account of ideal timing for deadlines.

Non-emergency situations will be notified with a day or two's notice, and approaching deadlines can then indicate the most appropriate time to convene. This will be early in the week for a weekly paper, and early in the day for a daily paper.

Ensure you have an adequate venue with sufficient seating for anticipated attendance and with sound re-enforcement if this would be helpful. Arrange to have suitable drinks available before and after the session.

Select your main spokesmen—usually one or two speakers and a chairperson—and then draw up an invitation list. Distribute invitations with adequate notice.

Brief your speakers well. If necessary instruct them to limit their comment to that which is approved by the national communication director for your church. Prepare a news release based upon the agreed and approved statement. This will be distributed to each journalist present, and sent to those who could not attend. Prepare your speakers for possible photographs.

Provide a solid table behind which the speakers will sit and place clear name plaques in front of each person. Leave a good amount of space between this table and the front row of seating to allow for photographers and sound-recordists to manoeuvre.

Keep a list of invitees and record an attendance list. Compare one against the other later. Send a copy of the news release to those who were invited but did not attend.

Introduce the speakers by name and position. The main speaker will then make or read an agreed statement reinforced by further comment from the second speaker if necessary. The Chair then fields or refuses questions as may be appropriate. The Chair should be seen to have the situation under control at all times, and concludes the conference formally.

A photo call may then follow, after which individual interviews may be organised if appropriate.

Section Four: Thinking Laterally

Chapter Eleven:

Opportunities Unlimited

As we seek to make use of local newspapers to help inform the community about the church, we need not be limited to submitting written material for the news columns, because there are several more options than that. These include:

- *News pictures*
- *Features*
- *Christian columns*
- *'What's On?' diary columns*
- *Letters to the Editor*
- *Display advertising*
- *Using news-writing agencies.*

This chapter seeks to explore these alternatives.

News pictures:

It is true what they say about a picture being worth a thousand words! Sometimes a picture is all that is needed to convey a story. Your eye is caught by the pictures before you read the print. A picture gives a page life and arouses curiosity. The days are gone when a front page was covered in nothing but text. Newspaper editors recognise our natural attraction to pictures so they employ them whenever possible.

Herein lies a lesson for the Christian communicator! People are far more likely to find interest in church news if it is captured in a picture than if it is just printed in words. This suggests we should seek to use pictures to advantage just as editors do. We must be alert to good photo-opportunities, and capitalize on them for effective communication with the world beyond the church.

Generally an editor will prefer to send a staff photographer to take pictures for his paper because he/she has a trained eye and can deliver the correct quality and type of print required to deadline. Only occasionally will a paper accept pictures directly from you. Nonetheless, it will help if we try to understand what makes a good news picture. This will call for some more personal homework on your part!

Go back to the copies of your local papers to evaluate the pictures they have recently published. Clip out the 'local' photos from news columns over the past month and assess them to see what makes them of interest. You will probably find that the best are action pictures involving people. **Static pictures with no people or people lined up doing nothing, tend not to make compelling pictures at all.**

You will also notice that dynamic pictures have a focal point, a centre of interest. The people in it are concentrating on doing just one thing. Your eye goes immediately to where the action is focused.

Consider this in the light of the Jim Woods story in chapter eight. A passport-style mug-shot of Jim would have limited appeal to the newspaper. But put him and his wife alongside his shell-scarred truck holding the shrapnel and pointing to a hole in his cab, and you have a compelling action picture that your local paper would be glad to use.

Part of the work of a PR secretary is to visualize opportunities to communicate news in pictures, and then to market those ideas to the local papers. You go about this by:

◊ Preparing a brief news release stating the What, Where, When, Who and Why of the subject, *and* the Where, When and Who of the picture opportunity.

◊ Delivering it to the newspaper office and speaking to the editor or picture desk outlining your photo-story.

◊ Inviting them to send their photographer or offering to submit a quality picture of your own.

If they opt to send their own person, be 'ready to go' as soon as he arrives. Make sure the key people and their props are on hand with no fuss, briefed to be paying full attention to the situation. Try to appreciate that the photographer is probably racing against a deadline and has other appointments to reach. Treat him or her like a VIP, assisting but keeping out from under his/her feet.

Introducc thc photographcr to the key people in the story. Give him a clear note (typed if possible) of the full names, titles and relevance to the story of each person included in the picture. Have a fact sheet ready to pass to him if required.

If the paper does not have a photographer available, or if for any other reason you need to submit a photo of your own, do a bit of homework first to see what format the paper will consider using.

You can do this best by asking the editor directly—*'What type of photograph will you accept from a non-staff photographer, if any? Will you only accept black and white prints? Is there a minimum size of print, such as 8" x 10" (200mm x 250mm)? Do you want the picture to be contrasty or grey?'*

You can also learn a lot from scrutinizing the pictures they have published in recent weeks. Go back to your copies of the local papers and try to learn from the pictures they have used.

may find yourself waiting a full week, by which time your story will no longer be news.

Identify the picture and its subjects precisely by typing the information and date onto a separate paper and taping it to the bottom of the photo in such a way as it can hinge up behind the picture. This is sometimes preferred to a label stuck to the back because an editor can read the caption details and simultaneously view the picture to see how it lives up to his expectations.

Generally you will need to be a very good amateur or a professional to obtain the kind of quality and composition of print that the papers require, but with modern auto-focus and auto-exposure cameras you may still be successful.

Take the picture outdoors if possible. Limit the group to two or three people rather than a crowd. Follow the rules given later in this chapter.

Prompt processing of black and white film is always a problem and you

Features:

'Features' are in-depth articles centring on a person, a group or a company, on an event, or on a place. They are usually researched and written by a staff reporter from the paper and will almost certainly include photos. But since 'features' are often triggered by an idea sent in by a third party such as someone in a PR role, you should be alert to this potential.

Newspapers are prepared to invest time and skill on their features, and it is up to you to grab the imagination of the features editor. This is how to go about it:

- Take a good look at the regular feature articles in your newspaper, so that you understand their style.

- Identify a subject in your church which may be attractive as a feature and prepare a Fact Sheet and a 'Feature Release' along the lines of a news release.

- Phone or visit the editor. Identify yourself and say you have a story he may want to develop as a feature. Explain the most interesting facts, especially those you feel will catch his attention. Give him your Fact Sheet and Feature Release.

- If he likes the idea he will take it from there by dispatching a feature writer in your direction. If he knows your work from past experience he may even invite you to write the feature yourself.

- If he does not take up the idea at all, never mind! At least you tried. Find the courage to ask the editor how you might improve your presentation next time.

Christian Columns & Comment Columns:

Some local newspapers carry a 'Christian Column' compiled by a staff writer or freelanced by a local Christian. If you locate such a column in your local paper you really should make the most of the opportunity to assist them with contributions from your church. Direct contact is the most likely key to unlock this channel. Write or phone the person who runs the column, asking how you may be of help.

The advantage of writing for a Christian column is that your copy is less likely to be discarded or heavily edited—so long as it is not written with partisan bias.

'Comment Columns' written under a banner such as *'Speak Easy'*, or *'Soapbox'* or *'Public View'* similarly invite local participation. Though not exclusively Christian, these may provide an opportunity for your church to make comment from a Christian perspective on matters of local current interest. Analyse how they are used in your local context and think of ways in which you may become involved in the debate.

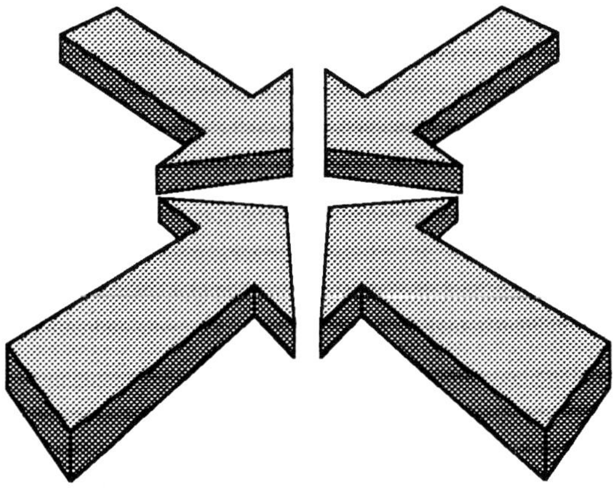

You need to be stimulating and lively, uncomplicated, relevant, topical, but brief. More than 500 words is probably too much. Convey a Christian perspective without indulging in Christian jargon. Avoid using Scripture as a sledgehammer.

'What's On' Diary Columns:

These columns conveniently list forth-coming events chronologically giving essential details in terms of the 'BIG 6' What, Where, When, Who, Why and How. Whatever the event your church is running, a bit of advance planning will provide the opportunity to have it posted in the 'What's On' Diary. Entries are usually published free of charge.

Always ensure that the data is complete —without the 'BIG 6' they won't know where to meet!

Papers usually do NOT accept diary data by phone in case details become confused. Submit a coupon from the paper, or prepare an information sheet. Mark it clearly for the 'What's On' column.

Do not assume that by submitting a news release to the editor the information will automatically also reach the person responsible for the diary column. These are two distinct functions within the newspaper office. So send a specific report to each party concerned. The editor will record your event in his desk diary to prompt him to dispatch reporters and photographers, whereas your dairy-release will be published for the public whether or not the editor uses the story in the news column.

Letters to the Editor:

In our society the 'Letters to the Editor' column has replaced the market square of ancient times where the public could exchange views on current issues. Thus they provide an important avenue of communication.

'Letters' offer an opportunity to express personal opinion not available elsewhere in the press. They offer a means by which *everyone* in the church can participate in a communicator's role.

'Letters' are very useful for:

* Correcting an inaccurate article, news story or previous 'Letter'.
* Bringing an issue to public awareness.
* Registering an alternate view, a Christian perspective on a current topic.
* Providing or 'filling-out' information about your church/denomination.
* Campaigning about an issue—whether pro-life, 'green', or whatever.
* Providing a chance to say 'Thank You' after an event, such as door-to-door collecting.

Study the 'Letters' in your local papers to identify the kind of material your editors have published. Think about which style communicates best.

This will give you a clear pointer as to how you can be successful. It will also make you aware of the many opportunities there are to express the Christian viewpoint.

Display advertising.

Few churches can afford to pay for advertisements in their local papers because of the high cost of the sustained campaign necessary to have any significant effect in the community.

However, there may be circumstances in which paid advertising is the only or the best method to communicate what the church has to offer its community. This would be the case when the church wants to publicize community programmes, for example.

In this case, call at the newspaper office and ask for their 'display advertising' rate card. They will always have a member of staff who can advise on cost-effectiveness and options relating to size, position, layout, frequency, etc. But you will need to obtain the services of a layout artist to compose and complete the artwork for the advertisement. A professional in the church may be able to provide this service, or you may have to pay for the services of staff at the newspaper.

The news-writing agency.

There may be a local news-writing agency in your town which will prepare and circulate your stories for a fee, but this is probably not cost-effective in many cases. The possible advantages to using these agencies are:

- News-writing agents are professionally familiar with the style and presentation of news most appreciated by the editor.
- Editors are used to receiving items from such sources. Their desks receive a steady flow of news from agencies every day.
- Agencies have the facilities to fax or E-Mail your item, and know how to select appropriate destinations for your release to optimize chances of success.
- Their livelihood depends on success, so they will be trying hard to succeed for you because they want you to come back. □□

NEWS PICTURES—THE GROUND-RULES:

1. The picture needs to tell a story. By looking at the picture the reader needs to feel something or to learn something.

2. The picture needs action. Readers are not usually interested in looking at static pictures that have no people in them, or that simply have people lined up doing nothing.

3. The picture should demonstrate what the story is about. For example, if the story is about Jim Woods and the risks of his trip to Sarajevo it needs to convey something of that.

4. The picture should have a centre of interest. The people in the picture should be seen to be concentrating on doing one thing—for example pointing at the shell scars in the cab, or presenting a charity cheque, or children up to their arms in paints at the Holiday Bible School.

5. The number of people in your picture will normally be limited. It is only rarely that a crowd scene has relevance—as in riots or demonstrations, or crowds watching a civic or royal occasion. Generally the picture should be limited to three or four persons. Faces in crowds become so small they are hardly recognisable. It is usually only professional photographers who can capture one or two faces in a crowd and make the picture tell a story.

6. There should be no wasted space in the picture. Move people close together even if they feel momentarily uncomfortable, and move the camera in as close as possible to the subjects. Do not leave gaps of emptiness.

7. Children make excellent subjects. People love kids. Therefore kids lend a natural human-interest element to pictures.

8. Watch your backgrounds. Watch out for plants or flags that appear to sprout from the heads of your people. Watch for distracting backgrounds. Watch out for flash-bounce off items in the background.

9. Strive for technical perfection. Make sure that your exposure is correct and that you have the centre of the picture in sharp focus.

10. Don't take snap-shots to your newspaper unless you also have the negatives which you can leave with them. The paper will usually work off a minimum 8" x 10" print.

11. Make sure your caption is thoroughly complete and accurate. All people in the picture should be identified by full name and title, and their position in the church or relevance to the story given accurately. Double-check to see that the '*5 W's and the H*' test is applied to the caption.

LETTERS TO THE EDITOR

HOW TO BE SUCCESSFUL!

1. Try to be topical.

Being 'topical' means basing your letter on a recent news item or current issue. It means responding to what is *presently* in people's minds and on their lips. It's about adding your comment to the 'live issue' of the day.

By definition then, this is going to call for a prompt response. If you feel the urge to write, do not put off the writing until some more convenient moment! Topics of interest change from day to day—sometimes they change by the hour. If an issue sits up and begs for a response but you delay, you may miss the moment and never get another opportunity.

2. Work at being relevant.

Put yourself in your neighbours' shoes and try to write your letter in a way which will appeal and be relevant to them. Think carefully about how you can say what you want to say without 'turning them off' before they have grasped your point. Use language which will draw them into your subject rather than becoming an obstruction. Quoting Bible for example, though appropriate amongst fellow-Christians, may defeat your objective because the man in the street is not on that wavelength. But do not be afraid of controversy or humour.

3. Identify your reference point.

Name the author and identify the original article and date of publication of any item which you wish to discuss within your letter. Summarise any letter to which you refer. For example, write:

Dear Editor, Regarding Mr Frederick Smith's letter, Newtown Gazette, Friday April 28, in which he raised the issue of bored teenagers roaming Newtown streets each evening . . .

4. Be brief and to the point.

A short crisp letter has a better chance of being published than a long vague one. Short sentences are easier to read than long ones. Every-day words are more attractive than extravagant or unfamiliar words.

Select one topic and stick to it. Decide one or two main points about the issue and limit yourself to them. 150-200 words is about the right length for one letter.

5. Be factual, be accurate and be courteous.

Always be sure of your facts. Double check them. Never make assumptions or rely on gossip. Be courteous in your choice of words. Your view will be less valid in your reader's mind if you use criticism, ridicule or sarcasm. Avoid being rude or disrespectful. Be gracious, and let the compassionate strengths of your Christian faith shine through even the most sensitive or strongly-felt discussion.

6. Let your reasoning be sound and your criticism be constructive.

When you have prepared your first draft, leave it aside for half-an-hour while you do something different and then come back to read it again. It may help to ask a third party to read your letter and comment on the soundness of your argument. Do not resort to subjective comment such as *'Anyone in their right mind has to agree that . . .'*

Be positive. Agree whenever possible. Let any criticism you are obliged to make be helpful, wording any comment that constitutes 'judgement' in a profitable and gentle manner, offering considerate solutions or alternatives.

7. When writing to correct error . . .

From time to time you may need to write to the editor to correct error which he has published in a news story, or to correct someone else's 'letter to the editor', or to offset error being broadcast by the media generally in respect of a given news story. If so, do it graciously, do it without delay, and inject some humour if possible. This will help take the steam out of the situation and give a positive and attractive impression.

8 Speak as a private citizen.

Generally you should write as a private citizen and member of the community rather than as a church authority. If circumstances suggest you need to write formally as a representative of your church, seek the approval of your pastor or national communication director beforehand.

Whenever you can you should write from personal experience and first-hand knowledge, quoting illustrations from your own life. This helps establish credibility in the reader's mind.

9. Type your letter or write legibly.

Most editors prefer letters which are typed but this is the one forum where a hand-written item will also be received well, so long as it is legible. It has been said at the BBC that one hand-written letter is worth a hundred typed letters because they prove real concern from the man in the street.

Make sure your presentation is representative, its grammatical construction sound, and its logic and content commendable. If you identify your church in your letter you place it in a position in which it will be subject to scrutiny, so be sure your letter will honour it in every possible sense.

10. Identify yourself by full name and address.

Always print your full name and address on your letter, and always sign it. An editor does not normally print anonymous letters. He will expect you to tell him who you are, and if you wish to have your name withheld he will do so if you indicate this clearly. Simply mark your letter *'To be published Name Withheld.'*

11. Don't overdo it!

Do not keep writing to the same newspaper on the same subject, nor too often to the same paper even on a variety of subjects. Regular readers will begin to think of you as a soap-box fanatic.

It is better to encourage other members of your church to take the initiative too.

12. Don't get discouraged.

Even if your letter is not printed, do write again when the right opportunity occurs. There will be other discussions to contribute to. Meanwhile, rest assured that the editor will have read your letter. He may have chosen not to publish it for a number of valid reasons. Perhaps he had too many similar letters. All the more reason to write again on another theme.

13. And finally

Always send your letter by first class stamp —you could miss the editorial deadline by posting second class. Keep a copy of your original and of any published letters in your scrap-book for future reference. □□

Section Four: Thinking Laterally

Chapter Twelve:

Utilizing Local Radio

Norman Iverson was a religious programmes producer for UK local radio. Completing his preparation one Saturday for his broadcast the following morning, he returned to his car which was parked adjacent to a local theatre. As he arrived at the car the theatre doors burst open and scores of youths poured from the building.

From their demeanour he realised that they were not on the rampage, but seemed to be young Christians emerging from a Gospel event of some sort. Intrigued, he went over to ask them and found that they had just concluded a Christian Youth Rally.

'If only I'd known!' he exclaimed. 'I could have come over and recorded you and done some interviews.'

'We didn't think you'd be interested,' they responded.

That was the bad news! But the good was that a few weeks later Iverson did visit their church, recorded them at worship and broadcast it as the daily service the following weekend. He told them, 'You are part of our community, and we want to hear regularly from you about the things that are happening in your church.'

There is potential for churches to contribute to local radio. This chapter looks at those possibilities.

'Live' church service broadcasts.

Let us start with what is perhaps the least likely opportunity—a live broadcast of one of your church services.

This is a major undertaking not usually done under the auspices of local radio. However, if you have a suitable church facility it may be worth your floating the idea with the pastor or national communication director of your church. He will normally need some attractive 'hook' to entice the station to take the idea on board, such as the contribution of an award-winning choir, musician, or renowned speaker. They will also need several months notice.

Immense planning goes into a live broadcast, from draughting the format of the service, to printing hymn sheets, setting up the sound systems, and a full rehearsal. But it is done somewhere every week and your church could win a place on the schedule.

Recorded church services:

Some local radio stations still broadcast a regular weekly church service though this is a practice which seems to have almost disappeared. The way to find out is to tune to your local station or look up their programme listings.

If they do such broadcasts the way to approach the possibility is:

- *Talk with your pastor and/or church board.* Ask whether they would be in agreement for you to approach the religious programmes producer at the nearest local radio station, with a view to them coming to record your church at worship.

- *Phone the religious programmes producer at the station.* You ought anyway to establish a regular line of communication with this person in the same way and for the same reasons that you work to build an on-going contact with the editor of the local paper.

  Tell them you are approaching them on behalf of your church in your role as communication secretary, that you enjoy listening to their church service broadcasts each week, and that you want to invite him/her to consider scheduling a service from your church.

- *Seek to arrange a meeting with the producer, your pastor and yourself to explore the possibility further.* You will need to have done your homework by listening for several weeks to their typical broadcast so that you can draft a suitable service proposal.

- *Remember the objective.* The purpose of this aspect of local radio programming is to provide an opportunity to join corporate worship for those unable physically to attend church. So the content of the service should be 'neutral' in a denominational sense, and should not seek to 'evangelise'.

The same procedure applies whether the programme is to be a worship service or a 'songs of praise' type of programme.

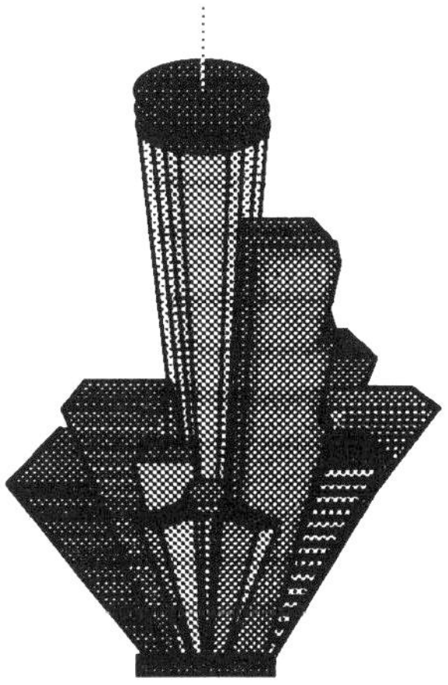

Church News and Diary Releases.

Local radio is very interested in local news and forth-coming events. Even when the station has no 'dedicated' religious programming they will carry news and stories from local churches in their regular current affairs programmes, and they will list forth-coming events in their 'diary' presentations. This means it is worth bearing them in mind whenever you are preparing a 'What's On' announcement for the press.

Once you have established a good contact with your local religious programmes producer, he/she will be expecting to hear from you fairly regularly. It is a natural expectation of such liaison, so do not be daunted. Give the presenter a ring from time to time to 'touch base' and bring them up to date with what is happening.

Be on the lookout for 'out-of-the-ordinary' stories or feature possibilities, and issue a news release or fact sheet as appropriate. Bear in mind that the various departments within local radio will not automatically share news with one another, so issue releases in triplicate—one to the religious affairs producer, one to the news desk, and one to the producer of the current affairs programming. Radio producers tend to prefer triple-spaced typed material to allow for editing notes etc.

Interviews & Features.

A news release or fact sheet on a lively human-interest theme is likely to provoke an interest for a radio feature or interview.

Submit the release to the religious affairs producer and then stand by to facilitate the interview. Take an extra copy of your release along with you and make sure the candidate for interview has had a copy. Some producers appreciate it if you suggest questions that may help the interview along. Let the interviewer and the interviewee have a copy of any list you prepare.

It is perfectly all right for you to suggest that the name of your church be mentioned at sometime during the interview, but it is not appropriate to mention it more than once or twice.

Above all arrive punctually for the interview appointment. If you are late you may spoil your chances for the future.

An interviewer may hint at the kind of question he/she is likely to ask, and it is well to frame some outline answers so that you can be sure of covering properly every major point you would wish to make. But do not take a scripted answer sheet with you because it will not work.

Sometimes it may seem that the interviewer is pursuing a hostile line of questioning, but he/she is usually only trying to anticipate the kind of questions the listener might wish to put if given opportunity, and most will not let you get away with wishy-washy answers particularly on themes known to be controversial.

But not every interviewer adopts the aggressive approach, especially in local radio programming where they are keen to maintain a friendly relationship with their community—of which you are a representative. They may push you hard but they will not deliberately humiliate you.

So the best preparation is to brief yourself first as to the type of questions that may be asked, and how you can provide pithy answers that avoid unfriendly questioning. You are permitted to take some notes with you to help cover the major points you wish to convey.

Some interviews will be pre-recorded and others will be broadcast live. The advantage of the former is that it is less stressful. The producer may also provide you a second chance to respond to some questions when your answer has come over a bit 'flat'. Be sure to arrive punctually for the recording. Other broadcasters will be wanting to use the studio too and if you miss your slot you could throw out the timetable for them.

When the interview is live, arrive about fifteen minutes before you are due on air to reassure the presenter that you are on hand and to give yourself a few moments to take in the situation.

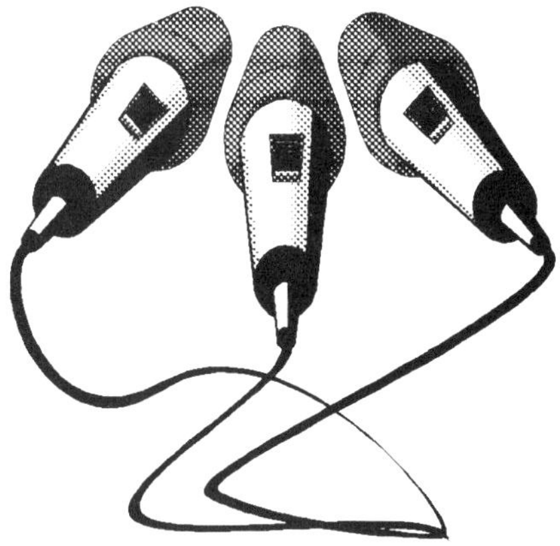

When your moment comes you will find yourself ushered into the broadcast studio, often while a record is being aired. You will have only a couple of moments of introductory chat with the presenter while he adjusts the microphone levels.

It may help him/her if you can write your name and the name of your church in bold print onto a card for their reference during the interview.

You may feel it a bit intimidating, but calm yourself with deep breathing and remember the interviewer is trained to help you relax and succeed with the interview.

Just remember to:

⇒ *Be relaxed as possible.* Try to be natural, and resist the temptation of putting on a phoney voice.

⇒ *Mentally prepare your responses.* You can do this by asking the interviewer what kind of questions he/she will ask. Try to anticipate the questions that the listener may have. Make mental notes of how you propose to answer the main questions, and how you might respond to possible interrogative questioning.

⇒ *Don't give complicated or confusing responses and avoid jargon-laden answers.* Think of the interview as a conversation over coffee with a work-mate. Use simple words. Put a smile in your voice! Be enthusiastic.

'Thought For The Day'.

Opportunities for local contributors to 'Thought for the day' (TFD) tend to vary somewhat across the country but do occur and they are worth enquiring after.

If your pastor or any other good speaker in your church is interested in being nominated to present TFD items, have them prepare three or four scripts timed to take about 1 minute 45 seconds. The script needs to flow smoothly, starting from some point you have in common with the average listener and moving to the inspirational point you wish to make.

Make use of your contact with the religious affairs producer at your local radio station and phone them with the suggested name. Send in the three scripts and invite them to contact you for a recording appointment. This is likely to be for broadcast at a later date perhaps a week or two away.

An excellent way into the TFD scene is to invite an interview or feature on some other interesting subject, and if that goes well suggest to your producer that this same spokesperson has some scripts for TFD if they should have opportunity to make use of them.

Hospital radio will occasionally be on the lookout for presenters of TFD items and it is always worth contacting its staff with this suggestion.

Radio phone-ins.

This is an opportunity to expose your church and its Christian views and principles which any confident member of your congregation can take up.

The first key is to listen to such programmes regularly to get a feel for the way the presenter handles those who phone in with comment. Usually they start by encouraging you to verbalise your contribution but some will press you hard if your contribution is not well thought out or substantiated.

The second key is to know what you want to achieve when you phone in. In other words:

◊ *Have something definite and worthwhile to say.*

◊ *Be able to defend your point of view and have answers to the main opposing views.*

◊ *Be coherent and polite. Don't rise to baiting or show anger. Agree to disagree politely.*

National radio may also present opportunity for phone-in responses. It is good for the nation to hear the Christian voice on the range of issues we face in the 1990s. So encourage your members to phone whoever it is that offers the opportunity for the 'voice of the public' to be heard. They may not publicise the name of your church but they will promote its standards and principles. That's what being the 'salt of the world' is all about!

Section Four: Thinking Laterally

Chapter Thirteen:

Writing for Your Church Paper

We've looked at communicating news from your church in terms of contacting the local secular media—particularly local newspapers but local radio too. Your purpose in that is to let the public know you exist and that you have an attractive church programme with which they can identify and in which they would feel welcome. However, there is another aspect to the work of the local communication secretary—that of letting your sister churches know about your congregation via your national church paper.

Your church paper is there to share inspiring news. It wants to stimulate flagging churches to help them keep pressing forward with the Gospel work. It provides an arena in which to discuss and exchange ideas about witnessing techniques and activities.

Communication secretaries commonly hesitate before sending a news report to a local paper. This is not always the experience for church-paper editors. They either hear nothing at all or they are overwhelmed by a stream of items, much of which has not been assessed by the 'News Value Gauge' and frankly is not worthy of being published. The difference at the receiving end, however, is fundamental.

The editor of a secular newspaper pays little regard to possible offence created by declining poor items. The editor of the church paper deliberately seeks to avoid turning down any report because he knows that to do so does cause offence and a loss of motivation. In consequence there is a risk that church papers may become victims of trivial reports which are of interest only to the members of a single local congregation.

Our objective in this chapter is to help communication secretaries to find common goals and interests with their church paper editor. These will include:

* ***Making the church paper <u>interesting</u> by submitting only newsworthy reports;***
* ***Making it <u>visually attractive</u> by submitting only the best photographs;***
* ***Making it <u>effective</u> in inspiring the whole network of churches to press forward.***

Essentially the same ground rules apply here as for news to the secular press. Before we begin to report for our church paper, we should ask *'Is this item actually interesting to anyone but me? Does it meet the expectations of the "News Value Gauge" suggested on p.26?'*

Some basic indicators may be helpful.

People are always interested in other people. Humans are naturally curious about one another. The church paper will want to exploit the better aspects of that curiosity. Readers enjoy news about other church members and like to hear about appropriate personal details. So make your items interesting by including information about ages, backgrounds, struggles, victories, conversion stories, etc.

Children are always interesting. The same rules apply. Adults enjoy wholesome, fascinating anecdotes about youngsters. So aim to emphasise interesting stories about what the children are doing inside and outside the church. Do not let this lapse into lists of names and tabulated achievements, as in reporting a Pathfinder investiture for example. It is all much more dynamic than that and readers are looking to be intrigued by kids having fun and enjoying their church. They like to see young adults 'coming good' in an hostile and corrupt world.

Try to connect the church with one of the 'live' issues of the day. The world is experiencing political, social and economic upheaval that affects every reader of your church paper They get help from reading how their church is responding to those factors. Abortion, 'green' issues, occult and New Age, disconcerting reports of activities in other Christian churches and your own—all of these things impinge upon the lives of your congregation and of the readers of the church paper. So make your items relevant by connecting the two whenever possible. If you find your pastor/church rarely touches on 'live' issues, have a chat together about it to see if this can be remedied—for the wider as well as the local benefit.

News will not often fall into your lap. You will have to go out to find it. Watch the active people in your congregation. Make contacts in all departments of the church. Attend church board meetings. Interview people. Take notes. Find active, lively stories by getting where the action of the church takes place. Don't attempt to summarise all your church's activities in a single quarterly summary but report each event as and when it occurs, while it is still fresh.

Some extra pointers:

- Most readers are going to be church members from congregations other than your own. Do not write very 'parochial' reports that will be of interest only to members of your own congregation.

- Do not report events that occur in all other churches too, unless something striking happens. For example, harvest festivals, visitors' days, Christmas events, and charity collections happen everywhere. In that sense, they are mundane. So reports about these regular episodes are only of interest if something out-of-the-ordinary occurs, by which a 'common' event becomes 'uncommon'.

- By all means report every baptism, even though these happen in every church, but to make your report interesting, single out some special aspect of the service or of the experience of the candidate which will arrest the attention of readers from other congregations. Usually the most interesting thing about a baptism will be a remarkable conversion story.

- Do not report anything and everything just for the sake of it. And yet, do not allow important events to go unreported.

- Avoid a 'blow-by-blow' method of reporting. Readers are not interested in the hymns you sang, the lesson you studied, who pronounced the benediction, etc. You are not writing the minutes of a meeting. You are focusing on fascinating aspects of things your church is doing, and recounting stories that will rivet the attention of the reader.

- Do not over report. It is unfair on other congregations if the church paper is asked to carry so much news from your church that others appear to be squeezed out. Over-reportage makes life more difficult for the editor.

Essentials of good news reporting:

CLARITY. Short sentences help to carry the reader along. Plan your piece. Have an outline before you begin to write. Re-read it, and perhaps re-write your article before you submit it. Remember, you are not writing for writings sake. You are *communicating*. Use words to convey a message.

KEEP THE READER'S ATTENTION. Your opening sentence should lure the reader into your piece. Tell a story; don't just stack the facts.

JARGON. Avoid denominational jargon phrases which turn off readers.

HIGHLIGHTS ONLY. When reporting the events of a special day, be selective in what details you include. The report should not begin with chatty comments about the weather or matters common to all church gatherings. Start with something punchy such as a quotation from the sermon or a quoted reaction from a member of the congregation, or biographical details with regard to the speaker.

GET YOUR FACTS RIGHT! Make sure your spelling of all proper names is correct. If you are providing a list of names (as for example with a list of baptismal candidates) use a uniform style—either Christian names and surnames throughout, or initials and surnames throughout.

Photography:

You may be tempted to submit photographs in a format that suits your own convenience rather than the needs of the church publisher, but that is not helpful in the long run.

The church publisher will be operating within the constraints of a budget. This probably means printing onto the most economic (and thus not the very highest quality) paper, and against cost and time limits imposed for each production phase. These limitations mean that to be most helpful you should be extremely careful and considerate in terms of what photographs are submitted.

Whilst it may be possible to get results off second-choice photos by utilising modern technology, it may be impractical or uneconomic to do so. The editor is then faced with the decision not to use your photo at all or to settle for an inferior result. Take good note of the following guidelines:

* First choice from the printer's perspective is a contrasty black-and-white print. This is going to be least expensive to duplicate and will provide a good-quality result.

* Second choice would be a very high standard, contrasty colour print. It will cost more to make use of and will give a poorer result, but one which is still aceptable.

* <u>Never submit slides unless specifically requested.</u> They are impractical from a cost and a quality perspective for normal black-and-white printing in church papers. They are usually reserved for full-colour work.

* The majority of photographs submitted to church papers are *under*-exposed. This is the most common fault. Since pictures degenerate in the printing process, losing perhaps 20% of their contrast, helpful detail may be lost. For instance, people's faces become less distinctive. For this reason very 'grey' photos don't work. Take great care with exposure and submit only those pictures with plenty of contrast.

* Photographs, like reporting, need to be *interesting*! 'Action shots' work much better than 'firing squad' pictures in which everyone is lined up facing the camera. Try to creatively vary the composition to introduce interest.

* 'Head-and-shoulders' pictures of the subject bring them closer to the reader. It is simply not necessary to have 'head-to-toe' pictures for the media. Take a look at your own wedding photos! The most interesting ones are close up, head-and-shoulders. Those kind of photos also work best for the church-news publisher.

* Take care with the composition. Make sure there is no distracting clutter in the background or foreground of the picture. Have a clear focal point in the composition to which the eye is naturally drawn.

Remember: If a particular report/photograph does not make it into your church paper, do not take it personally and get discouraged. Try again. And again. Along with your editor, you have the responsibility to make the magazine interesting and appealing. □□

Section Four: Thinking Laterally

Chapter Fourteen:

If it all Goes Horribly Wrong

You go to bed one night with everything in tranquillity, and you wake the next day to the news that something has occurred which will embroil your church in all manner of media pressures. Perhaps this news is local—the church has been gutted by an arsonist fire, or a member has been found dead in mysterious circumstances. Or perhaps the news is national, or even international—mission workers have been murdered or taken hostage by third-world guerrillas.

Or it may not be on that scale at all. An irate member calls you to complain that his name has been misspelled in the news item you have had published in the local paper—Jim Woods gets called Tom Woods or the Pathfinder Fair is listed in the Diary of Events to begin at 5.00pm instead of the accurate 3.00pm.

From the trivial to the devastating, things do go wrong from time to time, and the way to handle that is to prepare now for such eventualities. That is why it is important to nurture good media relations before adverse publicity intrudes. A good working relationship with the local media will make all the difference. Very often it may circumvent adverse news altogether because, knowing you, they will come for your comment before they go to print.

One of the best presentations on this subject for local communication secretaries is by Richard Thomas, in the chapter 'Dealing With Bad News' in ***'An Introduction To Church Communication.'*** *For more serious crises, refer to* ***'Crisis Management—What to Do When the Unthinkable Happens'****, written by Michael Regester and published 1990 by Hutchinson Business (UK).*

It is vital, whenever the repercussions of a news story have wider impact than the strictly local, to involve the regional or national Communication director of your church, who will take charge of the situation. If necessary, he will form a crisis management team with established authority to speak for the church, and select a spokesperson through whom all statements and responses will be issued. The role of the local secretary in this case is to render loyal and constructive support, and not break rank at all by making any personal comment to the press.

There are two types of unfavourable publicity that a church may have to deal with from time to time. One revolves around the publication of ***error,*** and the other around the publication of ***truth.*** The offending 'error' or 'truth' may also fall into one of two categories—

- Those in which the church is ***incidentally*** involved by association; and
- Those in which the church is ***directly*** involved as an institution or by the actions of an employee.

It may help if we illustrate these various categories.

INCIDENTAL ERROR.

This could occur when a person is wrongly identified as being a member of your church although he is not. Suppose your church is in the market square in Newtown. Protesters to French nuclear testing in the Pacific assemble on market day, using the steps of your church as a base. When traders realise their business is being adversely affected, they seek to move the protest away and assume the leader to be a member of the church with an inherent right to use the porch. When the media are called, feelings began to be expressed against the church though it was being wrongly identified in the matter. There was error, but it was indirect.

DIRECT ERROR.

This could occur in a case where a direct connection with the church is not disputed, but facts are misrepresented or speculative. In the Lindy Chamberlain case, some newspapers began to speculate that one of her beliefs might be child sacrifice—after all her Church was thought to hold unorthodox doctrines. The direct link to the church is not in question, but the doctrinal speculation was erroneous.

INCIDENTAL TRUTH.

This might occur when the church is inadvertently associated with a crime—a murder may have been committed in property neighbouring the church building.

The church is drawn in, not because of any suggestion of involvement in the crime but because it was associated by proximity to the villain. Any connection is totally incidental. It would be right to create an appropriate 'space', and to remove the church name board temporarily so that media coverage would make no unfortunate impression that the church could be associated with the crime.

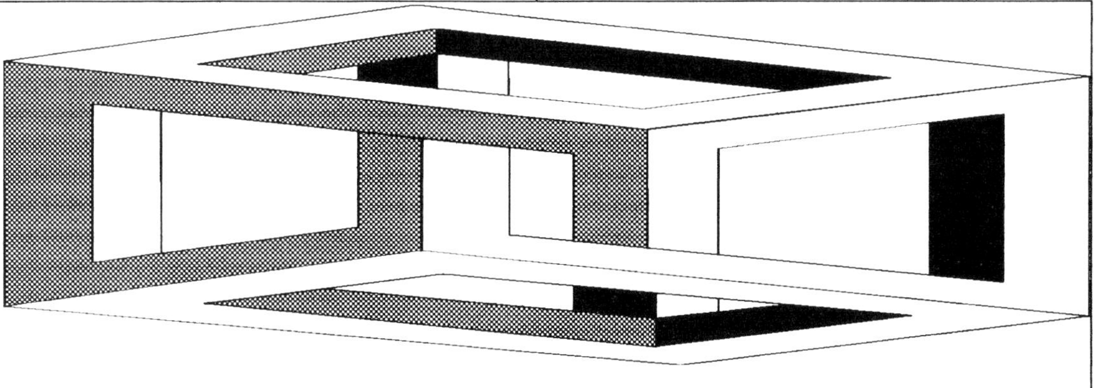

Direct Error—Or Incidental Truth?

DIRECT TRUTH.

This can happen when an event officially organised by the church ends in tragedy. A young man looses his life in a drowning tragedy whilst attending a camp officially organised and operated by the church. The question of possible negligence is not an issue, but the church is named by the media. It is truth, and the church is directly involved. It would be wrong to deny the facts. But any negative reportage can be limited by sensitive responses to the media and by genuine support of the bereaved.

Test your assessment of the following 'bad press' examples. Into which of the four categories would you place them?

* Church building razed by arsonist fire.

* Former employee sues church for unfair dismissal.

* Local treasurer embezzles charity funds.

* Claims that parish church habitually harbours illegal immigrants.

* Methodists reported as refusing blood transfusions on religious grounds.

* Member dismissed by firm because he declines trades union membership on religious grounds.

* Pastor Don Peters is reported as Pastor Don Perets.

Whatever variety of 'bad press' provokes our indignation, the role of the communicator is to keep the ship on as even a keel as possible by a programme of reassurance and damage limitation. This is best pursued by following a disciplined plan of action.

- **Plan ahead.**

Take seriously the need to build confidential links with the local media now and not wait for things to go wrong first.

Know precisely what your role is to be should anything go wrong. You are the local church communication secretary and you need only to respond to local media. If the 'bad news' is in the national papers you need not be involved except in correcting repercussions in the local press.

Your minister should be regarded as the 'Communication director' of your church, and you are the 'Communication secretary'. This means you do not have to carry the burden alone.

Be sure you know how you fit in to the 'Crisis Plan'.

Anticipate potential hazards. If you have reason to suspect there may be trouble brewing, get yourself prepared ahead of the impact.

- **Get things into perspective.**

Learn to put things into perspective. A minor spelling mistake in a name is hardly the end of the world, even though the individual may be momentarily disappointed. It certainly does not warrant making a fuss or unsettling a good relationship with the press staff.

When things are more seriously wrong than those minor details, don't go 'over the top' but follow the procedures given below. In other words, start with the gentle approach and tune up to firm action only if the situation demands.

If you can sense that a local story is going to blow up to national proportions, contact your pastor or national office without delay so that they may take steps in anticipation.

- **<u>Form a 'Crisis Response Team'.</u>**

This will usually consist of two or three key people:

—someone to manage the whole response (usually this will be the pastor or regional communication director);

—someone to give specialist input, such as a doctor, lawyer, accountant or the event organiser, as say in the case of a Pathfinder camp accident.

—someone to handle media contact (usually you, or the pastor).

The authority of the crisis team must be paramount. Church administrators should discuss plans in anticipation of such an eventuality and then allocate authority and 'power to act' with that team. There should be no intrusion or public contradiction to this authority. Differences of opinion should be kept confidentially behind closed doors.

If it is necessary to convene this response team, their duties will be to:

⇒ Find out all they can of the facts of the situation.

⇒ Try to identify the points of grievance.

⇒ Plan/co-ordinate what action shall be taken.

⇒ Prepare and issue an initial statement.

⇒ Keep a log of every action and reaction, filing copies of all correspondence, statements, releases, and newspaper clippings relating to the grievance.

- **<u>React with moderation.</u>**

In the first instance, make an informal approach to the newspaper pointing out the grievance and explaining the possible effect on the church. If the paper was in error they will usually correct it in subsequent editions. Newsrooms at local and regional radio and TV stations will modify their data and record a contact number for further reference on their computer item that relates to this story, and subsequent newscasts will normally be modified accordingly.

It may be appropriate to formalise your negotiations with the media by reinforcing your verbal contact with a written statement or release. 'Hard copy' in the form of a letter or release always provides a good reference point in cases of dispute.

In some cases a formal objection can be lodged with the editor or station manager requesting an apology or an opportunity for a corrective article or item. This should be reserved for incidents when the integrity of the church or one of its members is unjustifiably at risk.

- **The Press Complaints Commission.**

In cases when the media will not acknowledge your grievance or have grossly infringed upon the reputation of the church, it may be appropriate to approach the Press Complaints Commission, but this should be handled only by the regional or national communication director for the church.

- **Know when and how to say nothing.**

Sometimes it is best to remain silent. This would definitely be the case when matters are likely to become *sub-judice* or when they are personal to an individual who declines to authorise you to make comment on the matter. Respect that personal privacy.

Do not just say "No comment". Instead say something such as *'A formal statement will be issued when the picture clarifies.'* Explain your silence but resist the pressure to break confidence. Never volunteer names, addresses or additional information.

Understand clearly the relationship between the local communication secretary and the regional or national communication director of your church. When national events break in the news, contact your head office for an official statement. Make no comment to the press before doing so. Educate your local members not to be drawn into statements to the press which could be interpreted as in any sense representing the church.

- **De-brief after the crisis passes.**

Once the crisis is over, it is vital that the Crisis Response Team meet together again and de-brief as to the causes and effects of the grievance, the actions and effects of your response, and the lessons learned from the total experience. Keep these notes on record for future reference, and submit a full report to your regional or national communication director.